WILL THAT EVER BE FOLK?

Jane Arthur Dickson-Watt

authorHOUSE

AuthorHouse™ UK
1663 Liberty Drive
Bloomington, IN 47403 USA
www.authorhouse.co.uk
Phone: 0800.197.4150

© 2019 Jane Arthur Dickson-Watt. All rights reserved.

No part of this book may be reproduced, stored in a retrieval system, or transmitted by any means without the written permission of the author.

Published by AuthorHouse 1/10/2019

IISBN: 978-1-7283-8337-8 (sc)
ISBN: 978-1-7283-8336-1 (e)

Print information available on the last page.

Any people depicted in stock imagery provided by Getty Images are models, and such images are being used for illustrative purposes only. Certain stock imagery © Getty Images.

This book is printed on acid-free paper.

Because of the dynamic nature of the Internet, any web addresses or links contained in this book may have changed since publication and may no longer be valid. The views expressed in this work are solely those of the author and do not necessarily reflect the views of the publisher, and the publisher hereby disclaims any responsibility for them.

This is my story to be left to you Hannah, Alice, Emma, Rebekah, Katie and Daisy from your loving Grandi of Greshornish House. Isle of Skye, 1978 to 2004. (and Edinbane Hotel, Skye before then from 1971 and latterly in retirement at Sunart, Portree.)

It all started with my birth closely followed by me being christened the family name Jane Arthur Watt. The Jane and the Arthur come from my paternal grandmother. (her name was Jane Arthur Marshall I saw the initials J.A.M, on the corner of the double blankets, many times during my childhood as I trampled them with my bare feet in the warm soapy water in the "wally scullery sink on the blanket wash day) and of course Watt from my father and paternal grandfather and their forebears who were all Lanarkshire dairy farmers. Just to digress

Our lives all begin with our birth although none of us know anything about it. In my case I was told that it was a pleasant sunny summer's day, Saturday the 16th June 1934 to be exact, in the town of Paisley in Scotland. My parents and their forebears on both sides as far back as records have been collated, (so far that is circa 1712 but we could go further), were quite well heeled dairy farmers or cow feeders and contractors or whatever terminology had been used to describe the owning of land and the milking of cows and feeding of followers in big numbers added to these activities is the fact that my maternal grandmother's father was a Hay Dealer in Edinburgh in the early nineteenth century. They were all connected to or working in land they owned plus animal husbandry. You can see to this day there are areas in certain cities with a place Haymarket.

Back to Jane.

I insisted on making my way out of the womb between 2 & 3 weeks earlier than calculated by the nurse and doctor thus my arrival into this world produced an untimely, unwelcome surprise and consequently early small baby.

Untimely -------expectant mothers booked their private nurse for the baby's time of arrival but my mother's nurse was not available on the 16th June as my arrival date was about 1st to 7th July so mother, with me inside her tummy, was rushed into the nearest vacant maternity bed which just happened to be in The Barshaw Hospital, Paisley. The poorest joint in town where treatment of and facilities for pregnant mothers did verge on "workhouse" standards. Certainly there was no such thing as T.L.C. . (One paid for the doctor's visit and for all medicines so when you were ill you tried to get better without a doctor.) Many elderly people were well versed in natural and herbal medications and cures and were able to help a penniless mother in her time of childbirth.

Paisley is now (in 2004) well documented as a tough town but in these days it was full of wonderful friendly people known far and wide as the Paisley Buddies. It had rich farming land, even an Abbey, industrious hard working mill workers in Coats's Cotton Mills (The making of thread and cotton & the famous Paisley Pattern for shawls etcetera originated at this time and was renowned world wide. Almost every household in Paisley had a wooden box of beautiful cotton threads of all colours which had been gifted by Lady Coats. We were still using our box of coats threads in the 1960s)

Much employment and accommodation was guaranteed by Lady Coats for her mill workers. But people were poor because they had big families and the wages paid were minimal by today's standards. There were no government handouts. In 1934 there was no family allowance or sickness or unemployment or invalidity benefit or government financial assistance such as there is today so if you were poor or sick or ill or unemployed or unable to work for money and had no reserve of money in the bank you would just starve or beg from friends or relatives or go to the aforementioned "workhouse" To compound all the above conditions the country was in the middle of the great depression which you can read about. The Wall Street Crash of 1929 which lasted through the 1930's.

Will that ever be folk?

You can also read about the "workhouse" in David Copperfield by Charles Dickens.

Mother was quite nonplussed about this harsh situation, she knew the drill about giving birth to a baby as I was her 2nd child added to that she was well versed with the "calving of cows" and the milking of cows. Baby Jane, being before time, was small so dropped out like a pound of sausages expressed more quickly by the fact that the buxom nurse jumped on my mother's stomach at the 1st "push". As this strong nurse pulled me out she stretched my umbilical cord which consequently nearly pulled my belly button out of my stomach thus for the next 5/6 years I had to wear a rubber belt to press my "belly button" back to my belly.

Another problem with a small baby and a mother who is a good "milk producer" is the fact that the mother makes too much milk and the small baby is quickly sated leaving the breasts still full thus they get hard and excruciatingly painful and milk fever can set in because the milk is not being drawn off. (If I remember correctly in the cow's udder it is called mastitis)

Again Mother scored as she had the sense, ability, guile and "know how" to surreptitiously milk off this excess milk, secreted in her over full hard breasts, into the cloth and basin which was supplied in the morning for the washing of her face and hands.

(This aptitude on her part to parallel the human body with that of the dairy milking cow was quite amazing considering that she was the youngest child of an aristocratic dairy farmer who had spoiled her shamelessly until his premature death of a tumour in the brain in his forty-fifth year when she was 9/10 years old).

She had to hide behind her towel the fact that she was doing this dastardly milking trick as the duty nurse would have deprived her of this twice daily relief of the pain Evidently the other mothers in the ward watched her and they knew what she was doing, They tried unsuccessfully to do the same and daily begged, pleaded and implored mother while crying with the pain from their bursting full hard breasts "can you no milk me too missus?" there was no help for them. Bear in mind mothers were totally at the mercy of the nurse. You or the baby could die at her behest. Further to that the mothers were not allowed out of bed at all, not even to put their feet on the floor or go to the toilet for at least 10 days after the birth. (They were supplied with bed pans like a potty!!)

Blood stained sheets were not changed regularly enough thus the germs from soiling were allowed to multiply and many mothers died from bed fever brought on by dirty bed practises and lack of sterile treatment and being forced to lie there in the germs for 10 days. The nurses did their best and just did as they had always done through ignorance. Now in 21st century a new mother is asked to get up, to bath in sterile water, to go to the toilet etc. and have regular sheet changes.

After untimely comes unwelcome.

I was mothers 2nd child, the first was a girl (my sister Daisy). Farmers wanted sons so here was another daughter and a small, thin, premature piece of humanity at that. In fact when my Father first clapped eyes on me he looked in horror and amazement and said "will that ever be folk?"

Almost as bad as the boy named sue! What he did I guess was to make me tough. I was always small and thin but I was strong.

Part 2 of the unwelcome! There were only 13 months between Daisy and me and she resented me (just like Rebecca resented Katie in the beginning if you remember Katie got Rebecca's cot and chair etc. and Becky was not pleased and tried to pull her off or out of them if mummy was not there to stop her) Well that was how Daisy was with me and really Daisy was just a baby herself and did not quite understand why this small thing should get so much attention and use her things so she pulled and tugged at me and blamed me for everything even to the soiling in her nappies.

Part 3 of the "Unwelcome" factor Mother said I was an accident as she had been led to believe that while one was breast feeding a child and while one had no monthly menstruation one could not conceive. Well 1st she was breast feeding Daisy, 2nd she had no menstruation and 3rd she became pregnant with me.!!

The final blow I dealt my mother at my birth was the date and the day. The 16th June was the Saturday of the beginning of the Scottish Agricultural Show week. That year 1934 the Agricultural Show was in Paisley. All their friends, relatives, their whole known farmers world and his wife and children would have been there and not only was mother on the labour table but Daisy, who was only 13 months, still in nappies and my father being no "new age" father resented the fact that his wife was not there to look after this demanding toddler with him at the show. He was amongst farmers and cows maybe even "showing" some beasts. Then when he had to come back home (with this toddler) to all the farm and dairy work while mother lay in bed he was a bit resentful of her resting time and the presence of this despised morsel of humanity. It was entirely my fault. So Father was upset and mother missed the show totally.

I shall explain the Agricultural Show factor. In these days the A.S. went to a different town each year just like the National Gaelic Mod does today (maybe that will change too) Nowadays the A.S. is a permanent fixture at Ingliston in Edinburgh.

One did look forward to the year the A.S. was in ones home town and it may be only once in 20 years that that did happen. Added to that remember that in 1934 the chief private mode of transport was the horse and cart or horse and trap or horse and dog cart or the bicycle or shanks pony all very slow compared to the car so one did not go a far place like Inverness. It would have taken two days to travel from Portree to Greshornish. The only time you were sure you could attend the Agricultural Show was when it was on your doorstep.

{My father could have had a car and my mother would have learned to drive BUT my father's youngest sister Isobel was fatally knocked down by a car in 1911 while running across the road to meet her teacher, she was in her 7th Year. It was possibly the only car on the road for months/years but it killed his wee sister so from then on a car was a killing machine to my father and remained so till he died.

I may just mention now that his brother Arthur died aged 4mths in 1900, his sister Jane was 4years in 1901 when she died, his brother James was 1 year in 1901 when he died then Isobel in 1911(and Basil in 1918 in the 1st World War, The Great War and he was buried in France) None of the latter deaths are car related but the pains of all these deaths of his brothers and sisters never left him or his mother (my grandmother and all enhanced the 'hatred factor' of the car as a mode of transport.

Isobel is buried in Paisley Abbey Cemetery Lair 58/59

So you see father would not have a car. He loved the horse. It was slow and safe}

During the 1st world war farmers and their sons were exempt but the government demanded the services of one token son from each farmer. My father, by dint of his order of birth was the token son but his brother Basil offered to go in his place. In truth Basil died that we might live.

I digressed a little there for effect. Are you still following the story girls?

My home at birth was a farm and a dairy shop sort of place. In other words not only did my father and mother own, feed, milk and calve the cows look after all the animals including hens on the farm. They had a house attached to the dairy from which mother sold some of the milk plus eggs, cream and butter etc. So she was very busy with the farm work, shop work and two babies particularly Daisy who could run about and make mischief and a mess and blame it all on me this new, helpless, tiny unwanted baby.

I just lay there and slept and looked about. In fact I was a perfect baby the best ever and to get praise like that from my mother had to be not only true but well earned. Mother was not generous with superlatives but I managed to make her and my father overcome their resentment as I was no trouble. Mother said she could leave me in the pram all day and I was a happy smiling child (I still am) she just breast fed me then topped & tailed me and put me down. If you just think back to the crying and screaming all your sisters did at the baby stage and toddler stage, Hannah, and even when they were older you will understand how great it was for any mother but particularly a farmer's wife who was expected to do so much dairy and farm work plus sales in their dairy shop. (All with no electricity and no flush toilet or running water and no disposable nappies, no tins or jars of baby food.) I feel sure that if I had been a fractious baby my mother would have sent me back to the hospital.

There were lots of nice families asking if they could adopt me. I know one was a Lady Hamilton. But mother refused. I often wondered!!!! Well actually it nearly did happen the first morning (while still in the Barshaw Hospital) mother was handed a baby boy at 6am feed time, she was tempted to say nothing (she knew my father would have been delighted to have a boy but she did confess to the duty nurse that she had given birth to a girl. (Babies were often mixed up because the nurse took the new babies to a "baby nursery ward" during the night to let the mothers get some sleep. When the babies were not tagged or named mistakes could and did occur.

My father's first farm was Sergeantlaw, up the Gleniffer Braes, Paisley. (It was where he was born in 1894 and his father, my grandfather was there since 1850)

Sergeantlaw Farm was hard work for example getting out of bed at 2am every morning and drawing water by the gallon from a well to give a drink to 60 milking cows, 2 horses plus the house tea and toilet and all other uses like washing clothes or the cows' udders. The cows were milked (with the help from 2 maids plus his wife, my mother and his father, my grandfather) This said milk had to be sieved, strained, cooled and carted in big 20 gallon churns to George Street in the town of Paisley and be there on or before 6.am otherwise there was no sale for the milk as someone else had muzzled in and stolen the market for that day. One could not afford to oversleep or be ill or late otherwise one had to take all of that "last night and this morning" milking home and make butter or cheese and pour the rest down the drain or have a bath in milk!!! This was the time before the Milk Marketing Board came into being. The Milk Marketing Board gave all farmers a guaranteed sale for their milk and it was regulated by a quota system so you would state each month or year how many gallons you wished to supply to the board. The Board came to the farm gate to collect the churns of milk. It was up to each farmer to adhere to his quota just like your Daddy did with mussels sales to the Shellfish Marketing Group.

Apart from all that returning milk hassle there was the usual farm work of the season to get on with on the farm, the byre the harvesting, fencing, whitewashing, wall building,

Mother decided that this was no life and as my father was about 40 yr old when he married my mother and had been doing the above work since he left school at 9 year old she felt that enough was enough.(Yes you could leave school at 9 years and most children did especially farmers sons) and so mother wanted him to sell up and go to a more modern or more easily run farm also I guess she felt this was no life for her with no running water, no electricity and about 4 hours of work to do before you got even a cup of tea in the morning. As providence would have it this decision was taken for her.

My grandfather Basil Watt died in 1932 so Sergeant Law was sold to give my father his ownership of the farm which he had in partnership with his now dead father

A fast stop gap of a home was a farm house of Howood Farm still in Renfrewshire. Daisy was born there in 1933. Then we bought this Dairy with land in Renfrew itself from Auld Aunt Mary (my father's aunt, I guess sister of his father) that was where I was born in 1934. This old Aunt Mary borrowed £600 from my father when he resold the dairy, and conveniently never repaid it to him which fact stuck in my mother's throat for the rest of her life. (£500 was the price of a bungalow on the Glasgow Road, Paisley in the 1930s so that £600 would be worth about £600,000 or more today maybe one million

This said aunt reared Uncle Tom (my father's brother who had lost a part of his stomach through being dragged over a wall by a horse which threw him so he became a town boy, stayed on at school much longer than his brothers and became a draughtsman for Fullerton, Hogert & Berkley in Paisley and remained there all his life. He consequently became heir to the £600.

From the time my father left Sergeant Law Farm he and consequently we all moved from farm to farm to house to farm and so on for the next 12 years.

One of the lesser known migrations in Britain was of Scottish Farmers to Essex and Hertfordshire. To this day some 50% of the land in Essex is farmed by descendants of these said Scottish migrants. The first wave of this migration took place around 1900 and the second in the 1930's. (Eric Tinney mentioned this fact to Boyd and I when we were visiting him in Essex in 2005 that all the land around his house and town belonged to Scotsmen to this day. The land there is rich flat farming land)

My father set off for Hertfordshire in 1936 to join the second wave. He decided prudently when he arrived to first take a job at a place named Hitchen while sizing up the situation. I remember the place a bit as I was 2 years plus I don't know how much.

I remember and there was a barrel outside the door to catch the rain water off the gutters. There must have been a need for that water for us to wash and cook and clean etcetera. There was a big river at the bottom of the garden and we were threatened within an inch of our life if we went near it. And of course that was where we played as much as possible as children do. Daisy went to school there so she must have been nearly four years old and mother sent me to school with Daisy, although I was barely 3yrs, so that I would be company for and help to look after my big sister. When I got to that school I just played with a doll's house and dolls because I was not a pupil, no one was teaching me I was just passing the time. This was wonderful for me because we had no toys at home. Father would not allow mother to waste good money on rubbish. The nearest I got to a toy was a hot water bottle in the shape of little red riding hood and she had a red velvet cape and a red velvet hat which covered the place where the bottle top was hidden in her face. Daisy had one also, I loved her, took her to bed with me every night and cuddled her warm body.(No house had central heating so we were accustomed to dressing and undressing in front of the fire in the kitchen then rushing to our cold bedroom and cold bed with our hot water bottle. Strangely enough I know that that was the routine but I do not remember ever feeling cold)

My only sort of toy was a tennis ball so I became very good at juggling games from an early age. I used to pester mother to buy me a baby brother. I cannot think why. I think I just wanted to look after him. I really do not know for sure. But I did want a baby brother not baby sister. Perhaps I had had enough of the sister stuff.

From Deep South England we made our way back to Scotland because Father had been too late for the migration and all the best farmland had been snapped up.

The next stop over was Penrith in the Lake District.

That is where my brother David was born so we are at March 1938. I was 3yrs and a bit I guess and Daisy four and it was a house we had (not a farm) and we had stopped there to let mother give birth to her new baby I presume with leisure and peace. Father did work there as a cowman and contractor. Our stay there was only for months so it was possibly just to be nearer to Scotland because the next step was buying a farm in Scotland.

The house was in Clifton, near Appleby, Penrith and was quite modern and father was at home some days certainly he was there to look after Daisy and me while mother was "confined" which was the terminology used for being in bed to have a baby. Mother had the baby at home this time to let Father experience the "joys" of giving birth. She was in her own bedroom and she had her own nurse as booked and father did the running up and down stairs with hot water and all other baby and mother and nurse's requests while he kept Daisy and I, downstairs, well fed and full and happy with slices of bread and butter and sugar. I do not remember eating pieces and sugar ever before or since.

There was a change of diet which consisted of bread and butter and condensed milk offered sometimes. We had plenty of sugar and plenty milk and butter and bread so he did the best he could for us. I know he was no cook and his best effort at food for himself was "gruel" or "Pease brose" also the drinking of buttermilk and sour milk. He did not know what food to give to two little girls.

I was so happy that I had got my wish "a baby brother". I truthfully thought mother had bought him for me and I was so keen to wheel him out in his pram. I was not allowed even into mother's bedroom. Adults were very secretive about their body and body functions and children were never really told the full truth nor allowed to see very much. (Remember babies were found under a gooseberry bush in these innocent days or delivered by the stork.) I think a week or more passed before I could see my baby brother and when I did I was not allowed to touch or hold him. I now know why, at the time I was quite upset. I said nothing and no I did not cry. I knew crying was not acceptable.

We left Penrith while Brother David was still a baby and moved to Scotland. All our furniture was packed into a giant Pickford's Removal van. Father travelled with the furniture van and removal men. Mother carried David in a shawl while Daisy and I walked by her side with our hand luggage to reach the station as we were travelling by train. That was quite a 'trachle' for mother as Daisy and I were just toddlers and the baby was still in nappies. No not disposables like your mummy and her friends used. Nappies were in fact like towels which had to be washed and dried daily. Tell me how did you that on a train journey? Mother had no buggy (she had a beautiful large Princess Pram highly sprung like a carriage but it was on the furniture van) so all the necessary baby gear plus all our stuff had to be carried in her arms. Daisy and I did our best to help but when mother reached Glasgow Central railway station and got out of the train she was exhausted. There were railway porters who came to the doors of the carriages to help travellers with their luggage. The porter said to Mother "come here ma hen let me help you" she knew she was home. The kindness and the sound of the friendly Glasgow accent brought tears to her eyes.

Now it was a taxi ride to Dalmacoulter Farm, outside Airdrie, the home of my Uncle Jim and Aunt Jeannie and Cousin George Jack and cousin Ada Jack. It was great to be there. Uncle Jimmy Jack was one of my mother's big brothers.

We stayed at Dalmacoulter Farm while our next farm was getting ready for us. It was fun for me there. No school for Daisy or I so it must have been the summer holidays. We just enjoyed the life of luxury, a huge two tier Bathroom, golden taps, shower facility, beautiful big jaguar cars at least three of them one for George one for Ada and one for Uncle Jim. We were taken out almost every day to Airdrie or Falkirk or Cumbernauld or Slamannan or Ayr. Yes they were the racing set!! Greyhound racing at Falkirk (Uncle Jim owned Brockville Stadium in Falkirk and had shares in White City Stadium in London) so we were in the "owner's box" while there and felt like royalty. Horse Racing at Ayr, we were special and feted there too, as the Jacks were such constant race goers and owned race horses and greyhounds. We took 6 greyhounds in the Jaguar cars (with leopard skin upholstery) to and from the races. Everyone seemed to own greyhounds. All Uncle Jim's greyhounds were treated regally although they sometimes were sick in the posh car.

On one occasion Daisy and I were given a greyhound each to hold while they cleaned up the car. The dog collar was leather but the dog lead was of heavy chain and our dogs saw a cat and gave chase. The chain cut into my hand and drew blood and I was dragged across the flagstone kitchen floor. The greyhounds caught the cat and ripped it in two. I was so ashamed that I had let go. It was not my fault or the dogs' fault. They are trained to chase a furry little animal like a hare or rabbit and it is their job to catch it. On the race track the hare always eludes the greyhound so this time the greyhounds must have thought it was their birthday.

Uncle Jim owned coal mines and all his miners had at least one greyhound. It followed like night follows day that greyhound racing was big business in all mining communities.

Miners were dicing with death daily so I guess gambling with money was similar to the gamble of their daily life. They did love their greyhounds and the racing of them thus in a way Jimmy Jack gave them their income and their hobby. J.J. himself was always black like a coal miner and used to wash from his head to his waist belt in the huge "wally" kitchen sink. Even after he had scrubbed up his eyes were still circled with black coal dust. (I don't think the men in the family ever used that film star bathroom with its sunken bath and gold taps.)

He was very generous in every way and especially with his little sister's family. With his money he was careless he used to throw handfuls of his dirty black, sometimes torn pound notes on the kitchen table for Aunt Jean to wash and iron, repair and sort out he never counted it or asked where she put it. In fact she banked most of it in her own name. (Jeannie Cupples). He always made plenty more through clever purchases and deals. Life is a gamble and Jimmy Jack pushed all boundaries and won.

He gave my mother her wedding (to my father). It was at Dalmacoulter of course which was quite palatial and Jimmy paid for everything. There was one stipulation his only daughter my cousin Ada was bridesmaid and the only one. Mother had already booked Mary Kay, her friend in Grangemouth, to do the honours and Mary had already given mother the obligatory tea set expected from the bridesmaid to the bride. Mother returned the tea set and apologised to Mary and bought a tea set for herself which is the one in our glass cabinet to this day.

I digress again to tell you that Ada, his only daughter died from T.B. five years after we left Dalmacoulter. I think she was 24 years old. She was ill for years and her Daddy paid for the moon and stars in the planet to cure her but all to no avail. He sent her to a sanatorium in Switzerland for months, he built a revolving sun house in the middle of their lawn so Ada could lie there always in the sun when she was transported from Switzerland back home. Whether it was anything to do with anything Jimmy Jack died just months after his daughter. I guess it was a broken heart.

After he and Ada were dead and Aunt Jean had died later cousin George had to fight a court case against his mother's (Aunt Jeannie) 'will' to get possession of the money she has salted away in the name of Jeannie Cupples which was going to her Cupples family and her brother George Cupples who was not quite the full shilling but to whom Jimmy Jack had given a good home and financial employment all his adult life.

George then found that the safe which had been full of jewels and I mean full, Diamonds, Rubies, Emeralds etc. in Jimmy Jack's day was now empty so to get all that back and more the case went as far as the High Court in Edinburgh. I think people paid J.J. jewellery when they were down on their luck as he helped them out financially. Maybe even during the thirties depression when the banks foreclosed on people J.J. exchanged their jewels for cash money. Perhaps he bought jewels as they would retain their value better than paper money so maybe he just bought gold and jewels.

(I shall digress further to mention that Hannah met George Jacks wife in Sept. 2018 in the Golf club, Falkirk as we were there for Ann Douglas's cremation. I was bold enough to mention that his daughter Alison Harris was a Scottish Conservative member of parliament in Holyrood….. One of my bragging stories.)

Back to my story.

Will that ever be folk?

We all stayed at Dalmacoulter for months free gratis (well actually my father did labour for him) and Uncle Jimmy Jack gave Sandyknowes Farm, Cumbernauld to us and did not want any money for it. (He had two or three other farms), Mother would have just said thanks but father was too proud and insisted on paying for the farm. Mother was annoyed. Jimmy Jack would not have noticed the presence or the absence of the money. JJ was good at dealing and gambling and lady luck seemed to shadow him.

I shall just take a minute to compare the fortunes of these two brothers of my mother.

Jimmy Jack is well documented above but his older brother John was not so fortunate although he did try. For a start John being the oldest was heir to the family farm which was Airdriehill Farm, Airdrie then to Rough Craig Farm later. (the latter was burned to the ground but Airdriehill Farm is still there. I visited it in 2010)

John Jack decided to go off to Canada to seek his fortune pioneering. Unfortunately for him Ann Grey snared him into marrying her by saying she was pregnant and he was the father. It was a lie as she was barren and they never had any children. So when he went to Canada she insisted on tagging along with him. Whether he would have forged a future by going alone there we will never know. We do know that a wife/woman would have been an encumbrance in a pioneering man's world and she insisted on him returning home to Airdrie when the going got tough. There was a house and home for them with my grandmother (mother's mother) but the farming as such was non existent I suppose as all had been stripped of animals prior to John's trip to Canada. However John and Ann moved in and made themselves at home there while ousting his sister (my mother). She now had no home as the sun rose and set on John as far as my grandmother was concerned. John got his "chair", John got his place at the table, John got his "place" total. (Hence the reason mother was willing to allow Dalmacoulter to be her home on her wedding day as sort of pay back.)

The great depression started in the late 1920s and early 1930s so John came back to poverty but he was saved by his brother Jimmy Jack who gave him a job in his mines. He made him "Chief" He was the fireman which is probably the top job. So he managed to live comfortably for the rest of his life with land and property but no great wealth and no family. He died in 1978 (same time as my mother) a broken man.

His wife had predeceased him and all his property was in her name as he had assumed he would die before her and he had made out his will in her favour. She in turn as you do, had passed the property and land and contents on to her own relatives the "Grey" family when she died. The problem was she died first. Her relatives descended like locusts to claim their inheritance (remember John was still alive) and moved in to oust John from his home so as a tired old bereaved man he had to fight a court case to keep his possessions plus his own roof above his head. Actually it was his nephew George Jack the son of his brother Jimmy Jack who helped him to win the court case and throw the "Grey" relatives out at least until John died.

Who would be better than George to fight a family court case? George had had his own family problem for experience.

I could carry on with this boring saga but suffice to say some people get a good start in life like John and seem to work hard all their life and just make ends meet, some don't even make ends and others like Jimmy Jack grasp the nettle of luck and go boldly into financial dangers and become rich.

We moved into Sandyknowes Farm. It had been renovated, repaired, cleaned and scrubbed, papered and painted throughout, a pink bedroom, a green bedroom and a blue bedroom all with wall paper and matching borders. No home before or since had had so much renovation and decorating carried out prior to our taking up residence. I feel sure this was all instigated by Jimmy Jack. There was a big sitting room called the Good Room and we children were not allowed to go there. We all lived and ate etcetera in the big

Will that ever be folk?

flagstone floored kitchen with a large wooden table and a black grate on which mother did all the cooking and baking of girdle scones, clootie dumplings, oatcakes, scotch broth, lentil soup, stovies, curds and whey, boiled hen, stewed steak, mince and potatoes. All of these were my favourites except the lentil soup.

These were happy times. Baby brother was in his big pram and cried and cried almost as bad as Alice. Daisy and I took turns at rocking the pram to make him go to sleep. He cried so fiercely that he got a lump in his groin. Now he had to wear a belt sort of thing. He was just hungry and mother did not realise that she did not have enough milk for him plus her milk was not rich enough so when she started him on solids he grew like a mushroom and quit the crying.

Amazingly toys seeped through to him, a horse on wheels with a long handle, a wooden barrow, wooden bricks and other wooden toys. Daisy got a Fairy Cycle. I do not remember what I got (nothing I suppose) but it was not a big deal because I had started school properly and I used to sneak a shot on Daisy's cycle but my biggest joy was the fact that I was my Daddy's wee girl. When mother went to town on the bus she took the baby because he was too helpless to leave at home and of course Daisy was her little helper. (Two is company and three's a crowd). I was left at home I don't suppose I was much help to Father but I did as I was told. I was never bored. I tidied the house and cut my father's hair and ate porridge.

The hair cutting was an operation like mowing the lawn. He had a small cutter like a lawn mower and he started at the back of his neck and mowed a path right up over his crown to the front of his head. Then he handed the machine to me and said now cut the rest. Well the only method was to shave off all his hair. I usually left a tufty type fringe at the front if he had not ruined that too. He just wanted an easy care hair style. It seems he was thirty years ahead of his time but I thought it was awful. All men had a short back and side hair cut in the thirty's, forty's and fifty's and part of the 60's

I was not interested in the baby toys I wanted to read and write and count and look after my baby brother. I read some parts of the paper the People's Friend and on Monday we got the Sunday Post and Daisy and I argued over who would read Oor Wullie and the Broons first. I usually won because she had her cycle!! We were not allowed to have Comic Cuts other than the Sunday Post. Mother bought a gramophone (not electric we put in a handle and wound it up to play one record at a time. We had a fantastic collection of 78 s. records like the Laughing Policeman, Harry Lauder's songs and George Formby songs and many more even today I still know all the words by heart so must have played them most days, well we had no t/v, no DVD, no computer, no videos. We did have a wireless but it was all serious talks and news.

Cumbernauld is populated now with the overspill from Glasgow and re-housing of certain parts of Glasgow and has become rather an unbeautiful place in fact the shopping centre has been voted the place most deserving to be wiped off the map.

We went to school in Cumbernauld Station. This was a small Primary School with a headmaster plus 1 teacher. There was a Cumbernauld Village down at the bottom of the second hill on the Glasgow Road. Cumbernauld Station was at the top of the hill on the Road between Airdrie and Falkirk. The "Village" had all the usual shops like baker, butcher, dairy, grocer, post office etcetera. The "Station" had one shop only and it sold sweets, I guess it sold all sorts of things but for me it was sweets only as I used to buy my daily "gob stopper" there. The gob stopper was a highland toffee with a highland cow picture on the wrapper and I could get two of them for a ½ penny. (There were 240 pennies to the pound, 480 x ½ pennies or 960 farthings so I could have bought 960 highland toffee caramels for the pound. There were 4 farthings to each penny). Once you put the sweet into your mouth you could not speak. It was so large it filled your mouth and being toffee it lasted for a long spell of sheer ecstasy and ruined your teeth but we did not care.

Will that ever be folk?

It was a distance of about 2 miles from Sandyknowes Farm to Cumbernauld Station which was down hill from the farm. Daisy and I walked to and from school daily. I took pieces with me because I would not eat the school dinner. I abhorred the sight of the blood red beetroot running into the corned beef. Sometimes I would not eat the pieces either because the bramble jelly looked so awful when it mixed with the soda in the scone. It turned a black and navy blue colour as it had been wrapped and kept for hours. Mother got worried because I was such a skinny small child who could not afford the luxury of not eating. For a treat she sometimes met us half way between school and the farm. We ran up the hill and she brought pans, in a basket in the pram, down the hill so we could have mince and potatoes at midday sitting behind an old "stane" dyke in the field. Sometimes she walked to meet Daisy because she was bullied by a red haired tinker girl (a Mary Mc Phee) who lived past Sandyknowes up Fannyside Moor way. I was never bullied maybe I was so small and thin that I was invisible or was it because I was a good runner or fearless.

Life at Sandyknowes seemed so settled but not for long. Mother was so happy there. The farm was the right size for the two of them to manage without farm workers. Mother was such a lady in her dress and gloves and bag and hat. She loved going to town and could do that frequently be it to Falkirk or Airdrie or to visit her brother John in Chapelhall or the family of her brother Jim in Dalmacoulter. She could put us three to bed and leave us with dad while she went to the pictures. She had it all, her lovely family plus their son and heir for the farm. (All farmers must have a son.)

In 1939 Hitler a German leader first invaded Austria then Poland and U.K. had a protective agreement that if he invaded Poland we would declare war on him. War was declared in 1939 and lasted for 5 years till 1945. This must have been awful for my father because he was 20 when the Great War broke out with Germany in 1914 and lasted till 1918 causing the death of his brother Basil and hastening his mother's death. Here he was now just 46 and the whole world at war again with Germany. He would know what deprivation and restrictions would be ahead of us and he would have the flash back of how it was before. We did not know anything except that every day we were reminded that there was a war on clean your dinner plate, do not show lights at a window, and stay completely silent when requested. All windows had compulsory thick black blinds installed so that not even a chink of light would escape outside. All the signposts were removed. Think even on Skye how many signposts you read daily while driving along the roads.

These precautions were in place in case a German or any enemy landed from a 'plane or a parachute and tried to reconnoitre be it to kill or to spy on what protections we had in place to defeat the enemy. If there was no light to be seen and no road directions visible his map would be no use to him. Cumbernauld is quite close to Glasgow so the German spies would drop down by parachute to direct the enemy planes to where to drop bombs on the shipbuilding and industry on the river Clyde.

Rationing started then clothes and food and everything you wished to purchase became scarce or unobtainable. We were all issued with 2 coupon books one was for food and one was for clothes. We were allowed to use one coupon per week for the recognised articles of clothing or food. We were allowed 4 ounces sweets per week, 4 ounces meat per week, all small quantities like that of everything per week so we were all thin and healthy. I was quite unaware of this deprivation as we had plenty milk, butter, cheese, and mother had bought in large bags of flour and oatmeal so we had plenty scones and oatcakes and porridge. She had also stocked up with tins of syrup, condensed milk, and fruit. I remember carrying these tins up the hill to Sandyknowes from where we came off the bus at the bottom of the hill. It was sweltering hot days, the tins were very heavy and the string bag handle cut into my fingers but my method of alleviating the load and covering the mileage of road was to run a few yards then rest then run a distance again then rest and my rest places were in the shade of each tree as its shadow was stretching across the road. That way I kept pace with mother and Daisy who were also loaded with tins.

We had fruit in the garden, blackcurrants, redcurrants, gooseberries and apples so we had jam. We grew potatoes, carrots, turnips, cabbage. To this day I still eat as I did then, porridge, soup, potatoes and vegetables. We also had hens so we had eggs and boiled hen.

Farmers on the whole were the best fed during the war.

It was at this time and at this place that I had mumps and measles and was allowed to sleep in the bed settee in the good room. I guess it was also more convenient for mother as it was on the ground floor as she plied me regularly with hot blackcurrant drinks made from her home made jam.

There were limited amounts of paper. No toilet paper, no tissues, no wet wipes. We had cotton wool, towels, towelling nappies for the baby and we cut up the daily paper into little squares and tied the squares together into bunches with a small piece of string and hung that on a hook in the bathroom. We had various other methods of surviving every scarcity as it arose and we all became the masters of improvisation.

We were all given gas masks and all school children had to carry these always. They were in cardboard boxes with a long string to sling over our back with our school bag. Mother bought us a leather case for our box to keep it dry thus we had a leather strap to put our box over our back along with our leather school bag. We felt quite posh as we carried these gas masks everywhere. Well we were rich.

We all had to be registered and wear a means of identification. This would also be useful to recognise our body should we be bombed or get separated from family in an air raid. My number was SJP1 70-4. Daisy's was SJP1 70-3 Daisy and I had a silver disk on a moire band with our numbers engraved on it which we wore on our wrist always. The S was for Scotland and the 4 was to show that I was the

4th in the family and so on. Babies did not get a gas mask they had a sealed drum like thing which held the whole body of the baby and when sealed had a breathing section to prevent the inhalation of gas.

Once the war was in full swing and Britain blockaded, the British government was naturally very keen to grow as much food as possible to replace the non existent imports since most of the ships were used to carry soldiers and ammunition for the war effort thus farmers were zoned and forced to plough by government demand. The men with the pinstripe suits and brief cases decreed that Sandyknowes Farm should be ploughed. Father was doing just fine with his grassland plus a little hay and root crops. He knew that it did not make sense to plough this steep stony ground. He was a good farmer thus decided to sell up and move to another farm rather than comply with the ignorant bureaucratic demands.

This was the last time I saw mother dressed as a proper lady with her edge to edge coat, smart kid skin leather gloves, and galoshes to cover her shoes from the rain and mud until she reached the streets of town when they were tucked into her carrying bag. The silver fox fur was hung over her shoulder, the umbrella at the ready and as a treat I'd get one square of her ubiquitous Fry's Cream chocolate bar. She was so keen to be lady like in dress and mode and here she really was. The proximity to Dalmacoulter farm meant she could visit her brother Jim and his family and neighboring farms of Waterside and the Paisleys, also the Reids of the Tunnock where there were opportunities to dress properly apart from the frequent town visits and cinema evenings. Daddy was a happy baby sitter as long as we stayed in bed and slept while mother was out.

Now we were on the road again in the spring of 1941. So the above style all died or was placed on the back burner. Muirhouse Farm was our next home. It was beside the river Moose and seemed to be on the edge of a moor in the vicinity of Carstairs. The school for Daisy and I was Lanark Grammar School which was a big school which took primary and secondary pupils. We had to get a bus to school so it must have been between 5 and 10 miles away.

During the war children were taken from their homes in the big cities and sent to the country to escape the blitzes or bombings by the Germans. Naturally these said children (who were named evacuees) had to go to school somewhere so they flooded the country schools. Primary 1and 2 (that included me) went to school for a half day only to make room for the evacuees to go for the other half of the day. So one week I went to school by the school bus in the morning and finished school at lunchtime got the service bus to take me to a drop off point from where I walked the further two miles home along the moor side. The alternate week I walked to my pick up point two miles along the moor road late morning and spent the afternoon in school then came home with Daisy in the school bus at 4 o'clock. I became used to my lonely solitary walks for miles along the moor side and used to pick bog cotton and stick it up my nose always striding along briskly singing marching songs which I must have heard on mother's gramophone. The only one I can remember now is the "March of the Cameron Men." of which I know all the words to this day and the Red River Valley. My songs were all sad about pain, heartache and regret although I was happily singing them.

The farmhouse was big. It had the ubiquitous "good" room into which we were forbidden to go. We had electricity but it was produced by a generator so when the cows were being milked by machine morning and night the lights in the house became very dim.

We bought this farm from two bachelors (the name that springs to mind is Frame brothers). They left a roughness of everything on the farm and in the house even to a large chiffonier in the big flagstone kitchen with drawers full of boot polish and cleaning stuff and farm and animal ointments and requirements. There was brand new Ford Model T car in the farm garage which they wanted to leave. The brothers had not used it at all as fuel was scarce and I guess they saved their ration for the generator. Mother bought the car from them with her own money for 100 pounds and was being taught to drive by them. As petrol was rationed there were no driving tests so you simply mastered the gears and the hand signals and drove off into the sunset! Father said no way. He was scared stiff that she would kill herself, flash back to his sister's fate. Father was a placid man, madly in love with mother, but he could put his foot down firmly when the occasion arose and this car was it. He was no gambler, certainly not with danger. He was also thrawn and men were all powerful in these days. Mother was furious but had to abide by his rules. He had killed stone dead her only chance to move into the modern mode of transport. She was renowned for her fearless handling of the horse. She would have been a competent driver.

This farm was off the beaten track and a car would have made life bearable for Mother and us. That finished Muirhouse or Moorhoose. It was sold and another move was in progress. This time it was West Redmyre Farm, Allanton, Shotts, Lanarkshire. This farm was the antithesis of the previous one as it was right in the middle of the village. The council house tenants bought our dung for their garden (it was all about grow for Britain) and Daisy and I took it up to their gates in a wheel barrow. That shows how close they were. If they did not get the dung they stole it out of the midden at night. Everything had to be locked up or it took feet and walked be it a shovel or a horse. Seems they cut through fences to get into the fields to play football and showed little respect for the growing crops. The soil was rich the crops were good and the hay and corn was not only essential to feed the milking cows but also was almost impossible to obtain by any other way, like buy in (as the crofters do today on Skye.)

I can remember my baby brother (aged 3 ½) cycling around the wall of the aforesaid midden showing off his prowess on his new tricycle still wearing the kilt outfit he'd donned for the visit to town. At least he had a soft landing when he lost his balance. Mother was none too pleased. I was just glad I was nowhere near him thus could not be blamed.

Will that ever be folk?

At school Daisy got infected with Scarlet Fever A great hush was introduced as sale of milk with these germs on the premises was illegal and the dairy would have been closed or Daisy would have had to be put away. Daisy stayed in bed and we all closed ranks. You see with the farm being right in the village people came to our door for milk so our home life was open to the public like being a goldfish in a glass bowl.

It was then for first time I pretended not to notice Mother slipping her washed hen eggs into the can or jug of milk on the quiet. Sometimes she made butter and it too was sold at the door using the same method of subterfuge. If she had been caught or reported it would have been a heavy fine or imprisonment. There was a war on!!! Did I tell you?? Everything was on ration and mother was not a registered egg or butter supplier only registered to sell milk as per quota. Also I guess these sales were what one would call "pin money" for the wife. Work that out for yourself. So we were very rich cash wise as the milk cheque came in each month from the Milk Marketing Board who collected the allotted quota of gallons daily in 20 gallon cans from the farm from father so that kept him financially happy. The door sales were partially illegal. (called the "black market".) During the war the "black market" thrived in every necessity and luxury of life. Once you deprive people they will find a way to break every law in the book. Think back to prohibition in the States in the 1930's. or the "SS Politician" which sank off Barra during the war. The name of the game is outdoing officialdom to survive and making money to buy more than just bread. One sometimes resorted to barter that was not illegal but had no adrenalin flow and was much less stressful.

For my part I loved the school. It was just a short walk up the road for a change and I always had company from the miners' sons and daughters and the occupants of the council houses. I was between 6 and 7 yr. old at this time. It was there I got 4 or 6 teeth extracted in one visit one day when the school dentist called. Our parents were just told that the dentist would attend school tomorrow so each child must bring a big red hanky and a scarf. (every man had at red and white spotted hanky which was used for carrying lunch or wiping things) The red hanky was to soak up the blood and the scarf was to prevent the cold from reaching the holes in your mouth. This was all very practical but gave little or no tender loving care. There was no choice of maybe having a filling or two, oh no, it was extractions only and no mercy.

This was where I had the joy of having a boyfriend, my first. He was the brother of one of my pals and I was very friendly with Bill until he tried to kiss me and then I took fright. He was 8 yr. old. He was most serious. As soon as he heard that we were to be leaving the area again he insisted that there was a room for me to stay with him in his house. His attentions were quite oppressive. I think little boys of that age can be quite intense. He became such a problem to me that I had to hide in the girls' toilets at playtimes and run like the wind home so that he would not catch me to kiss me. I was glad we were leaving Allanton to escape from Bill. Mother and Father too were happy to be leaving thanks to the theft factor and all the other problems they had endured owing to the proximity of the farm to so many desperately needy people.

We moved to a cottage on the Earl of Bothwell's estate at Auchinleck near Ochiltree in Ayrshire. We must have left at the May term in 1942 because it was summer while we were in Auchinleck. The cottage was in the trees on a private road leading to the big house of the estate. I do not remember much about the school. I do know it was Auchinleck Public School to which Daisy and I walked as usual. Although we were changing schools so frequently I was never bullied nor did I find the lessons difficult. Every school in Scotland must have used the same books and all the teachers must have been cloned to allow my transition from school to school to take place so seamlessly. Mother cycled to Ochiltree for the shopping as necessary

Will that ever be folk?

as we were not on the bus route but I guess it was a healthy and cheap mode of transport. She just left David at home but locked outside.

Very soon I became covered in spots and it transpired that I had caught scarlet fever from Daisy. My infection was quite mild or so I thought as I would not stay in bed as expected. As a result I was put away. I landed in Old Cumnock Fever Hospital. It was one of these large stone buildings to be found in most Scottish towns which had been gifted by some benefactor like Carnegie. I was a bit home sick for a day and then I started to run the joint. As I said I was not ill and all the spots were on the wane but I could not go home until the danger of infecting others was over. I helped the nurses and they were a happy bunch who sang all day. The current song was "There'll be blue birds over the white cliffs of Dover tomorrow just you wait and see. There'll be love and laughter and peace ever after tomorrow when the world is free and so on. We all thought the world would never ever be free from Hitler and the Nazis this was the period of our darkest hour, 1940, so Mr. Churchill said.

In hospital we were given bread and margarine for breakfast and tea and at mid day we had soup. I was starving most of the time. Mother and father came to visit only once and brought me fresh strawberries and fresh eggs, butter and home made girdle scones but the nurses took them for themselves so I told mother not to bring me any more. Actually the nurses could not give me such rich food as it would have been unfair to the other children. All the boys and girls had their hair shaved off in case or because they had head lice. My thick hair was left in tact as I had no lice, my fever was almost over and I managed my hair by myself. I felt quite special. The nurses parcelled us up into bed at night so tightly that my toes were in danger of breaking so I slackened off the sheets a bit when they had gone. After "lights out" time I fell asleep and had a repetitive dream about falling over a cliff soon I fell out of bed with a thump on the hard linoleum floor. The bed was quite high and the mattress seemed to slope downhill when I lay on my side at one side so next time I'd lie on the other side but I seemed to be permanently sleeping on the top of a hill down which I rolled each night and fell on the floor. Each time a nurse appeared and shone a torch calling out angrily, "who's that out of bed"?. I scrambled back into bed as quickly as possible and did not confess. It was a big ward probably more than 20 beds so by the time the beam of the torch reached my bed I was back in place pretending to be asleep. I guess if I had left the sheets tightly wrapped I would have been cocooned in bed like the others. I'm sure the night nurse knew it was me. When it was time for me to go home I was quite nostalgic. That's when I decided I shall be a nurse one day. Many years later mother negated my choice of career with the unforgettable words. "It's the last bloody job. You'll be stanin (standing) on your feet a'day.

The war raised its ugly head again when an armoured battalion was billeted in the big house and over a period of hours a succession of tanks, armoured cars and field guns trundled past our front door. Two of the soldiers from this regiment had become displaced and hid in a ditch so that they could come into our house. Mother was wary. I could feel that they were not welcome but one had to put on a friendly face. They wanted to use the bathroom, have a drink, and just see children and home life. They were Italians who offered us a drink of alcohol, then left. Mother kept the door locked at all times from then on and I sensed a certain foreboding or fear. We would be on the move again to another stop gap.

Our next house was 14 Haldane Terrace which was the last street on the right as one leaves Balloch on the road to Stirling. Balloch looked good even in the middle of a war. The river Leven as it left Loch Lomond was crowded with brightly coloured house boats. Mother was quite nostalgic about the Loch Lomond area as she had spent many happy days there in her youth working at the Inverbeg Inn in the 1920s. The only way hotels in remote areas could have milk (fresh or otherwise) was by keeping their own cow. Not everyone is able to milk and manage a cow so mother found a niche

Will that ever be folk?

of indispensability as dairymaid. Not only did she supply all the milk for the hotel and a few neighbours but also all the by products e.g. cream, butter, crowdie, buttermilk. She was so important that she was official staff and could swan about in a black velvet dress and a string of pearls during the evening.(Her dairy work took her an hour or two in the morning and an hour or two at night so she had a great deal of free time) For entertainment she helped in the dispense bar serving scotch on the rocks, scotch and soda, gin and it, vermouths and many other old fashioned drinks, well by name only. This gave her the chance to broaden her social knowledge and horizons and meet people.

I do not know what father did in Balloch. There were farms nearby so he possibly worked on one of them. If he was in a house as opposed to owning a farm he would always take some sort of farm job otherwise he was as tight as a clam financially. Mother occasionally took some peace work there too to get her "pin money" again. I remember Daisy and I were shawing (taking the shaws off with a sharp sort of knife) turnips with her. I thought I was O.K at it but maybe not. It must have been fall as there was always frost in the fields. The mornings were cold and damp and as David said "unremittingly miserable" with constantly frozen hands. Fortunately the misery was short lived and we would be on the road again but not before I mention that since coming out of hospital I had been infected with impetigo on my face, of all places, (maybe that is the only part of your body where impetigo manifests itself) which I had caught from some of the children in there and had to have my face treated with gentian violet (a purple/blue cream). What a sight and what a punishment for a little girl of eight years. That was not all I had caught head lice in hospital too. All this appeared after I was out and home. Now I had my hair shaved off, yes mother left me with a fringe and some hair at the sides to cover my ears. I was always so sensitive about having my ears covered. I wore a woollen hat to school and just kept it on my head while in class. No one seemed to be aware of my plight at least if they did they said nothing. Even I myself do not recall any feelings of misery and my hair grew back again quite quickly.

The Sunday night treatment from now on was not only the usual bath and hair wash but our heads were soaked with paraffin (seems the paraffin loosens off the nits, just as well nobody smoked! But bear in mind that all homes were heated with an open coal fire and the mode of lighting was by candles, oil lamps, gas lamps or tilley lamps all of which required a naked flame to ignite them) then all our heads were thoroughly and repeatedly combed with the lice comb which was a two sided comb with two sets of teeth of varying widths. Mother combed out these offending beasties with great skill and squashed them with an audible crack of expertise between the middle of the comb and her thumb nail. This was a brutal, unsightly and dangerous but most efficient cure. It worked. I never had lice or impetigo again. I would add that the carbolic soap stayed with us at hair wash time just in case.

Our next home was a beautiful bungalow with a generous garden all around it plus a large garden shed full of antiques including a sword. Our address was Moss-side Cottage, Wester Boghead, Lenzie. Half of our garden was in Lanarkshire and the other half in Dunbartonshire. This was an affluent area. Mother tried to get me into Hamilton Acadeny as a semi fee paying pupil but I fluffed the entrance exam. Maybe I was too young. I guess it was quite easy but I was not prepared. Anyway father would have baulked at the cost. We were in the wrong zone for Lenzie Academy so we ended up going to the zoned Auchinloch Primary school for our home address. The upside of all this was that all three of us walked to school together and there was no broken days or half days. Life was leisurely and mother and father must have just enjoyed a well earned rest from work and flittings. The neighbours were great for me. I had a friend in one of the piggeries near by and our parents used to visit others.

The Watt genes could not suffer this sloth for long and the misery of living with my father in his state of no cash flow would have been too much for mother so although she enjoyed the ladylike life she did not think much of this unnecessary and untrue poverty. We were soon on the road again to find a farm and more importantly a cash income. Father had thousands of pounds but if there was no money coming into the home he was loathe to wastefully spend any and especially on us children. This meant we got the necessities of life like food and accommodation but no luxuries. Mother loved her extras and was pleased to have the opportunity to pay for them with her own ingenuity, mostly black market.

Whatever the real reason with the coming of spring we moved to Bishopton (outside Glasgow on the A8) The farm was Craigmuir Farm owned by a chap Whiteford who worked and owned another farm near the Red Smiddy on the same A8 road. Father seemed to be like farm manager and the house we had was tied to the job. It was huge with a large flagstone kitchen and scullery containing a large metal table like piece of equipment (seems it was an Anderson shelter), a sitting room, a good room and three large bedrooms upstairs. Daisy and I slept in a double bed which occupied a tiny space in one of these rooms. We could have had 2 eight some reels in the remaining emptiness. We crept up to bed in the dark each night. Sometimes when we were in the throes of uncontrollable laughter and giggles as little girls are with little or no provocation we were threatened within an inch of our life if we made any noise. I was not sure why until we were dragged out of our sleep in the cold in the middle of the night, told to put on our coats and shoes, wrap up warm, get downstairs to the big cold stone-floored scullery and crawl under this big metal table. This performance became almost a routine as the sirens seemed to scream most nights. We soon learned to keep a small suitcase there all the time as that table would be our last memory of life should a bomb land on or near the house. The sirens screamed and whined and the searchlights streaked across the sky making the sky seem like daylight while we lay and shivered in our shelter cuddling our only meagre possessions until it was all over. Similar to Cumbernauld, Bishopton was close to Glasgow and the shipbuilding on the River Clyde which landmarks were prime targets for Hitler and the Germans. Hence the nightly attention Hitler bestowed on the area surrounding us poor mortals.

The school was pleasant enough. It had no outstanding star quality for me. I remember a teacher telling me to wipe that grin off my face. (I think she had reprimanded me for something and I had smiled nervously from embarrassment as I usually did when being put in the spotlight. This made her think I was being defiant.) I added fuel to her fiery anger by wiping my face. Well I thought she meant there was a mark on my cheek. I did not know the word "grin". I would be doomed from then on. Sometimes it was beneficial to have a father who was continually lifting sticks and moving.

I had friends in that school with whom I swapped transfers and scraps. These scraps were like paper angels, cherubs and other beautiful paper people. It was a harmless past time governed by innocence and minimal financial outlay. All our activities had these qualities. In the playground we played peevers, did skipping with a long rope which was held by a girl at each end. All the other girls in the game formed a line like a queue so that each one of us could run through the moving rope. If you fouled up your run then you took your turn to hold one end of the rope. We had bouncing ball games if anyone could produce a rubber ball. Remember there was a war on!! Rubber was at a premium as it had to be shipped in. We had great material limitations and no aspirations of grandeur but life always seemed to be happy.

Mother used to take Daisy to Paisley or Glasgow on the bus which passed the door on the A8 as Daisy was so capable and could help her with the shopping she also took David as he was the baby and would get into mischief. The theory of "two is company and three is a crowd" kicked in again so I was left at home. No Alice I did not whine like you used to do. You always want the same as Hannah. I did not get to do or have the same as Daisy and I did not think to ask. I just knew I would be left at home. I quite enjoyed being alone in the house I was partial to tidying, scrubbing and polishing. I was proud of the fact that I was allowed to make lunch for my father. That was easy as it consisted of potatoes washed and boiled in their skin and served with butter, salt, milk and cheese if we had any. He came in from the farm work and seemed quite pleased with my effort. I was only nine. But that was the age my father was when he left school to work in the fields.

The time of leaving Craigmuir Farm was instigated by a tragedy of unforeseen dimensions.

My brother, David, waxes lyrical about what he saw and heard but I saw nothing. It was all over by the time I arrived home from school so my knowledge is as I was told. Father had put all the cows and stirks outside into the field opposite to give him a chance to clean the byre properly, an operation which took place every day at the same time. Dairy farming is so slavish to accuracy of repetition and routine and boy do the animals know this as it is they who call the shots and demand to be milked, to be fed, to be let out and to be let in. There are variations in the apportioning of blame but the gate was left ajar (possibly by the men who had been spreading manure in a field all week) and the young stirks who knew that their troughs would have feed in them when they were allowed back into the byre took the chance to charge back into the byre. For a start father was not finished his preparation and was not ready for them to return to their stalls in fact he was in the walk way shovelling cow feed from the big steel killer to the last of the troughs. The floor was wet as it had just been washed and hosed down. The killer/kilner was heavy and on wheels, father was at the far end of it so when the stirks rushed in they sent the killer straight at him at speed. In his desperation to avoid its onslaught he slipped and fell with his feet in the air and the back of his head coming into heavy contact with the sharp edge of the grip (like the kerb at the edge of the pavement) as he landed and that was the last he knew.

He was in great pain but by the time he reached hospital in Paisley he was unconscious and remained in that condition for about 6 weeks. Mother visited him regularly but I saw him only once in that time and I can remember noticing how handsome he looked. His skin was so white, his cheeks were pink almost transparent and his hands were beautiful. I had never seen his hands other than work worn and rough with heavy lifting and working in cold, wet and frosty conditions.

After the five weeks and three days he gained consciousness and a few days later he was released from hospital. He was not a fit man but he could not have restarted work any way where he left off as Whiteford had found a replacement for the Craigmuir Farm work, The cows had to be milked twice daily as usual. We were offered alternative accommodation in a small house nearby as a stop gap till we could leave. We were not welcome to stay in this cramped accommodation so we had to move as soon as possible. It was tough for mother with an invalid husband and three young children all at primary school to be finding that she was homeless with no cushion of the government hand outs like you get today. One had to be resourceful and just get on with it. There was always the work house or poor house looming.

Now we were on the road, this time to relatives again, the Drum Farm near Bo'ness overlooking the Firth of Forth. The Stewarts of the Drum's connection was the fact that an Aunt of fathers had married a James Stewart. They had a vacancy for someone to do their milk retail round. Mother was an expert in this line with the horse and trap and we all helped as best we could maybe we were more of a burden. I suppose father did something but we knew it was only a stop gap. He had money and the fact that mother was earning meant we had ready cash to spend without upsetting father's carefully guarded large bank balance. There was a house on offer in the deal plus coal, potatoes, milk and various other farm produce. It was summer time here so we had strawberries and tomatoes in abundance. We seemed to settle quite comfortably where ever we found ourselves living. This must have been due to mother's ability to pack, unpack and home make at speed. The boxes containing the fine bone china, ornaments, crystal and glasses were never unpacked. To this day even I retain an aptitude for pleating plated and saucers in between folded newspapers prior to packing them into boxes.

We always found a school to go to but this one neither shines in nor clouds my memory with happiness or misery. It would have played its bit part in keeping my education abreast of my age and class requirements. We all seemed to manage our school work admirably.

Bo'ness was a minor port protected by a few barrage balloons. The Forth did not seem to have the same interest for Hitler's army as the Clyde hence I do not recall being pulled out of bed to shelter from air raids. It was not a poor town but the sight of children running around bare foot would give an impression of poverty albeit summertime. There were back to back rows of houses whose water supply was supplied by some old lion headed hand pumps in the streets.

Very soon father was signed off by the wonderful insurance doctor. His name was Dr. Arthur, he will be dead a long time ago but he did us a great financial injury and what he did to my father and consequently to us was criminal.

By way of easing himself into a farm of his own again father bought what I would call a smallholding. (Like crofts on Skye but usually you own your smallholding whereas you rent your croft) The address was Rigghead, Avionbridge. (Near Slammanan and Falkirk and Bathgate and Armadale.)

As David put it we think father had always dreamed of being in the position of living off his interest. Maybe he thought this would be the time to give it a try as he was still recuperating although that wonderful doctor had signed him off. We could manage to live financially with produce from the ground, 30 hens, one cow, a horse called Flicka (called after the film My Friend Flicka) and the soft fruit available in season. Daisy and I used to enjoy riding Flicka bare back when out of sight of parental guidance and restrictions.

The house was adequate and we even had a bathroom and flush toilet but there was a down side the water had to be carried from one of the rain barrels at the doors. Worse still there was a well and it was a real Jack and Jill type so we could have this cold clear spring water whenever we could be bothered to drop the bucket down that deep hole then suffer the agony of winding it up to the top again.

Having a horse was permissible, having one cow was allowed but the number of hens had to be carefully controlled. Britain at that time ran a command economy and all egg producers had to be licensed and supply their eggs to an Egg Marketing Board. With fewer than about 30 hens we were probably within the law but the precise number of hens was a carefully guarded secret and mother sold our eggs at the door to the neighbours on the black market.

The cow, when it arrived was dismayed to find that it was alone in the field with only Flicka as a companion and longed to be with the cows in the field opposite. She plucked up courage to join them and took a flying leap at the fence. Being a milk cow she had not accounted for the size and weight of her udder which caught on the fence and grounded her before she could clear both banks of the burn thus crashed into the higher side and broke her neck. Apart from the financial loss of the cow there was the added expense of the removal of the beast plus the vet's fee, the forklift, the tractor and the burial. Now we had to make a nightly trip to Waugh's farm for our milk.

We were fortunately zoned to Westfield Primary School which entailed a walk of about a mile then a short bus journey. I say fortunately, since the closer village of Avonbridge was unacceptably tough and if we had found ourselves in conflict with any children there we would have had to suffer the uncontrollable wrath of these Wild West type fathers who lived only half of a mile from us.

Daisy sat her qualifying exam (eleven plus) and passed into "A" GRADE. The Watts (or probably more strictly the Jacks, mother's side of the family) had always held themselves in high esteem thus there was no surprise at Daisy's intelligence and ability. However much father might try to restrict us financially we were always brought up to feel rich, capable, and clever so that we were expected to effortlessly do well at school and seamlessly pass from grade A to grade A.

Father's tightness kicked in again when mother bought the school uniform for Bathgate Academy for Daisy. He was furious and threatened that he would rescind her partnership agreement if she showed such unnecessary extravagance again. Mother knew that he would do just that and maybe more. She was by now sure that the damage to his head was manifesting itself not only in epileptic fits but also by making his judgements have a certain irrationality. We were warned not to upset him lest we found ourselves on the wrong end of his temper. Fortunately he adored mother so she had no problems but he had a short fuse with us children and he would allow no money for luxuries for us. I knew how to work him but I knew my limitations. Daddy's epileptic fits started to take over our lives as not only did we not know where or when a fit would take place but also mother wanted one of us to be with or near him all the time he was outside so that he could be eased into a soft place to fall safely and would be supervised until it was all over. None of us had nursing skills but we sure had to be fast learners of how to cope.

This was a rather leisurely period. Daisy and I rode the horse. I learned to ride mother's bicycle without her knowing (it was a racer with curly handle bars) and when I was proficient daddy let me ride his bicycle. I knew that was a "special" (Daisy was forbidden) so I was delighted although it was difficult for me to negotiate that cross bar on a gent's bike as I was only 10. We picked rose hips from the hedgerows by the pound and took them to school. There was at this time a campaign to improve our levels of vitamin C and we were paid two pennies per pound for them. This was good money for us and father got in on the act with gusto and supplied us with about 10 pounds of rose hips per day. There were 12 pennies in one shilling and one shilling was quite a substantial sum.

There was a pair of high button boots in a shop window which I coveted. I was so upset that mother did not get round to buying them for me considering it was she who had attracted my attention to them and created my zeal to own them. (Children are so selfish and self centred) was that I realise how impossible it was for her to cope financially when daddy was so "thrawn" about taking money out of the bank I could weep at my unreasonable whining.

We had a Christmas there and the usual orange, apple, raisins etc. were in our stockings but Aunt Mary (mother's sister from Tealing. Dundee) sent a parcel. It was like manna from heaven. In it there was a leather shoulder bag for Daisy and one for me and a beautiful yellow satin dress with net overlay and a gorgeous wide pink ribbon round the waist which flowed down the full length at the back. Aunt Mary was very clever with her hands and had made them all especially for us plus many more things for David and mother. We posed about with these gifts and would not have called the king our cousin. Whether mother wanted to or not we will never know, (maybe she would have preferred to read a book), but most evenings (except Sundays) in the winter here she played Snakes and Ladders, Ludo and card games like snap and whist with us while daddy went to bed at dark. We had great laughter and competition and in retrospect it was such quality time with the family such as is not seen in your modern homes with your T/V's, DVDs computers and smart phones and ipads which are all so impersonal and uncommunicative. It was wonderful of mother to make us so happy when she must have been crying inside.

Mother also took a job as a dishwasher and or usherette in a cinema in Falkirk or Bathgate so these few pennies she earned were used to give us the odd luxury without father seeing. These jobs

Will that ever be folk?

were at evening time so Daisy and I were in charge of Father and brother David who was only about seven. Today she would have been prosecuted for leaving such young children alone in the house so we were on our honour to be very careful and good.

Father was seeing his local doctor who was giving him pills to reduce the fits and mother (who was willing to be a working mother and had had to put her shoulder to the wheel on many occasions before) was at the end of her tether and sick of the grinding lack of money.

The time had come to move on. We were all delighted to find that we were returning to a full scale farm of our own. Little did we know that this doctor had been economical with the truth.

Our new home was Cannonholm Farm. It was wonderful situated in the valley of the Clyde supported by rich verdant farmland. With about 100 acres of this land it dwarfed Righead's 12 acres. This land included about 2 acres of mature orchard and some 3 or 4 acres of alluvial flats fronting on to the River Nethan on which Mungo Sinclair, the previous owner had grown blue cornflowers and strawberries to sell to the shops. Stepping stones on the river on our land took one across to a hamlet with the unlikely name of Tillytoodelum. The River Nethan is a tributary of the Clyde and the nearest villages of between one and three miles away were Auchenheath and Kirkmuirhill. The M74 motorway now thunders past these villages plus Lesmahagow, which was the nearest town.

The farm was fully stocked with implements, grain, fodder and animals including a grey mare called Nancy, a large chestnut Clydesdale and most importantly some sixteen milking cows. Apart from the farmhouse, there was a byre for the cattle and a dairy for the milk, a stable for the horses and extensive other barns and outbuildings including one which had its own built in threshing machine.

There were of course some snags. Most of the land was steep and hence difficult to plough with horses and suicidal with the tractors of the time. But with dairy cows the ploughing factor was not a big problem as fodder could be bought in from the produce of local arable land. The private farm road leading to Auchenheath was about a mile long and steep too in places. Parts could be icy and hard to negotiate in the winter. The byre most curiously by modern hygiene standards lay through one thin door immediately next to the farm kitchen, while the dairy lay across the yard. There was also surprisingly, considering our business, no electricity. This importantly meant that there was no option, (twice daily), but to hand milk all sixteen cows.

The farm had a milk round, and retailed some forty gallons of milk daily to the village of Auchenheath and the small town of Kirkmuirhill. Mother always did the round with Daisy's help. This involved loading the churns onto a gig each morning, yoking up Nancy and driving off to town. The customers supplied their own milk receptacles for receiving the milk which they left outside their doors or they brought their jugs to the trap to have the milk measured into them through a tap on the biggest churn.

The milk of course was not pasteurised or otherwise treated. It was sieved and cooled before loading it into a churn. But the Ayrshire cows were tuberculin tested and their milk was creamier than the milk from the Friesian cows. By the standards of the milk of today our milk was unbelievably fresh and really creamy. Generally we despised store bought milk sold by our competitor the Co-op whose milk had forgotten what a cow looked like and had to have additives to disguise the fact that at root it was already decayed and rotten.

Mother would also make butter if there was any surplus milk thus she could supply fresh buttermilk to her customers. Remember we were still under rationing restrictions so our customers were grateful for any farm produce we could offer. Even the routine of the eggs or butter concealed in the milk can again reared up in our life.

Although the war was declared to be over life did not noticeably improve. Labour was in power and in love with rationing

Will that ever be folk?

They even at this time introduced bread rationing, which had been avoided for the whole duration of the war. The ration was not very large either. It was the equivalent of four slices per person per day, perhaps only two slices per child. In reality this was all very theoretical for us as we had our own milk, butter, oatmeal, potatoes, turnips and eggs in abundance plus strawberries and apples in our orchard in season. We children sometimes ate the cow's cake, maize and treacle the latter was in a drum with a tap at the bottom which we could turn on to catch some on a cup. This was not allowed but what child is perfect.

Slowly things were changing like the arrival of the Canadian Apples from British Columbia which were red inside and out and had the most overpoweringly delicious apple smell and flavour. Bananas had not arrived yet to us but we did hear stories about them and how children had died through eating two or three bananas. Although we did not know this the fact is that it would be another six years before rationing would be completely over with the worst punishment of all being that sweets were the last food to be plentiful in supply in the shops.

Back on the home front we were suddenly astonishingly rich. This was real. Our turnover on thirty or forty gallons of milk at four pence per pint would be around £10 per day at a time when soldiers were on 3/6 per day and Willie our 18 yr old farm labourer was on less then £3 per week. But apart from that it made a difference that the money came back home in a leather shoulder bag in coins and notes every day and had to be counted and banked. At that time with limited documentation how could any tax inspector check up and tell exactly how much was in the bag. Now mother, as she was the keeper of the bag, could buy whatever luxuries she wanted for herself or for us without having to ask father do draw money out of his precious bank account and without having to declare all to the government. Well we deserved it we all worked as a team. The earning of this money did involve child labour. Now the trouble was we had little or no time to go to the shops to spend the money and even our visits to the cinema was a thing of the past.

As I said every one of us was working. Mother did the dairy and milk round with Nancy the horse and milk trap. Both mother and father milked expertly and at a great speed and father had also started ploughing. Daisy was a tower of strength. She almost immediately became efficient with all the customer requirements and importantly those who had paid and those who had not paid.

Both Daisy and father excelled in mental arithmetic (although father had left school at nine years old) and Daisy who was at this stage nearly only eleven carried in her head all sums and amounts of money due from each customer on mother's milk round thus she could double check the books. Unfortunately as Daisy was so useful she was quite regularly kept off school to fill in the gaps and on one occasion we even had a visit from the truancy officer. For my part I did all the housework that was ever done and I did a local milk run with Willie on a Saturday morning. Willie did the run by himself on foot every morning when he carried two big cans of milk from which he measured out the ration of pint or ½ pint for customers to the houses within walking distance of the farm. I was with him on Saturday to collect the weekly payments not because Willie was not trusted, although there may have been a bit of that, but more to help him with my arithmetic skills and my family presence. There was a certain word mother used quite frequently to describe my ability. For abbreviation we shall say A.B. at this point later I shall explain.

We still went to school in Auchenheath. It was again possible to walk there; sometimes we got a lift with mother in the gig part of the way although we always walked up the steep hill out of the farm yard so as to lighten the load for Nancy the horse. I do not remember much about the actual school but it was pleasant enough. The headmaster was a Mr Graham who taught two classes in the one classroom. Every morning he held an assembly at which we all said the Lord's Prayer. A small number of pupils stood outside during this

Will that ever be folk?

looking through the door, then all trooped into the classroom when the prayer was over. These children I learned were Roman Catholics.

One morning shortly after starting this school, I was surprised to see Nancy come galloping up the street past the school, with the gig bouncing along behind her. Mother then appeared running at least fifty yards behind her. She was normally a wonderful horse, but something or someone had startled her and off she went. Fortunately she was soon caught and the milk round continued with milk shakes all round. Not quite true!! We did not know the words milk shake.

One day early in January 1946 it was decided for the first time to operate our built-in threshing machine. This was a combined operation for the whole family. Father, whose health now appeared to be very good, played a central role running this, cutting the sheaves and feeding them in carefully to avoid blockages, making sure the grain bags did not overfill and so on. My little brother David was up on the top level of the barn, throwing sheaves down into the feed tray where father could reach them. (We had no health and safety snoopers or regulations.) Willie was clearing straw and other things. I helped with the tea and food for the men. All went well and at the end of the day everyone was well satisfied. A big price was still to be paid and how.

Next night father had an almighty fit and did not get up the following morning. He was sleeping in the box bed in the kitchen for warmth and convenience for work and nursing. The bed was beside the black grate which always seemed to have a fire in it. We were usually out of bed early but this morning it was five o'clock. Daisy helped mother and Willie in the byre with the milking and I stayed with father. I remember holding a mirror to his open mouth to test if he was breathing as he was so still and quiet. I went down to the byre and told mother. I said I think Daddy is dead. It was all so matter of fact and we were all so practical and resourceful. The doctor was summoned. No one made a fuss and we did not scream or shed a tear. We had to get on with the job in hand. Mother was now on her own with one hired hand of 18 years plus three children all under twelve years. We had to get ready for school, do our food, and help mother with the cows and the milk routine. Cows are hard task masters and show no mercy through hell or high water they must be milked morning and night. Our grieving would have to wait for an appropriate time when alone and each would do it his/her own way. No public display of screaming and wailing.

That day went through in a blur. David went to school on the gig while mother and Daisy were doing the milk round. I stayed at home with Daddy and the doctor and all the other people who started coming and going. Willie did his milk round then he was back to do all the byre work on his own. When Mother and Daisy came back at about 11am Daisy and I set to doing the milk dishes which was our terminology for the washing and sterilizing of the huge twenty gallon milk churns, coolers, buckets and all such stainless steel equipment which was used daily in the dairy and all of them were really heavy for us. I had difficulty reaching into the bottom of these churns to wash them properly without falling inside head first. Then we had to turn them upside down and hoist them into the steamer chest for sterilizing. Remember milk production is a strict task master which demands super hygiene and cleanliness as snoopers are always on your back to report any fault or mishap on your part and milk is a perfect medium for bacterial multiplication and threat to the customer.

I digress to say we were not paid. Farmer's sons and daughters worked from 7 year old or earlier to keep the roof above the head and the belly full. No matter how rich one was property and land wise cash in hand was hard to find unlike the café or restaurant trade.

Outside help was difficult to obtain even when affordable. The war was over in 1945 but demob was not complete and many of the men and women who had survived were shell shocked, or broken in body and spirit or just recovering from their ordeal as best they could with no experience, or thought as yet of future employment.

Mother would have carried on the farm if we had been older. This was January 1946 and I was 11, Daisy 12 and David 7 years old. Farming was all we knew but her concern for us was uppermost and there was no option but to get the selling scene in motion again as soon as possible. Sheep farming or hill cattle farming would have been manageable but this constant grind of milking 16 cows morning and night by hand, all the sterilizing routines of not only equipment but also highly perishable produce, (remember there were no fridges or deep freezes and in fact no electricity so you had the added problem of lamps to fill, wicks to trim and globes to clean all of which were dangerous feats for children to do but we did) all the customers to get their milk ration correctly, two horses to feed and yolk, three young children to feed, to kit out for school. All of these responsibilities were daily; some were twice or three times daily thus unable close off for a few days till you had sorted out your life and regrouped the troops.

Mother was a tower of strength. I think she worked robotic ally all day then at night she slept fitfully but each morning she said to herself something dreadful happened yesterday. The horror of what had happened and the change her life would take from now on had not quite hit her and father's death was not mentioned. We all rallied round mother. I think when you lose a parent you grow up instantly. For a time all your selfish childish needs and requirements are put on the back burner. Crying about hurts and disappointments in a childish way was over. We had minimal toys before this tragedy and our pastimes were usually work and the like but now that grounding matured overnight to an unforeseen reality. We all put our shoulder to the wheel and helped mother to make it through each day.

Mother had so many seen and unforeseen arrangements to make without a phone, fax, mobile or computer and from a remote farm without pigeon post or telegram. The relatives had all to be notified and all the funeral arrangements to be made while daily doing all the cows and milk and children etcetera as detailed previously. The family and friends whom she managed to contact all came and the funeral was held at the farm. I had tidied the house, made the beds and prepared the kitchen and big room where the coffin was lying and helped with the food and catering arrangements while Mother, Daisy and David were out on the milk round.

I guess the funeral was at 12 mid day as that was the only suitable time. Daisy and I carried on with the dairy work while the service was in progress then after a reasonable time the relatives all started to drift away. I could hear the occasional sentences floating past my ears from the yard as each relative said his farewell and all of them seemed to be peppered with and what will happen to these wee weans. Uncle Tom and Aunt Lilly came to the dairy to say hello and goodbye to Daisy and I and Lilly offered to take me away to their home now and adopt me. She and Tom had only one son, Basil. (Tom would have loved more children but would not put Lilly through that punishment again. She had had a breach birth. Nowadays when the baby is in breach position for birth they do caesarean sections if they are unable to turn the baby round but poor Lilly had the primitive torture of having the baby pulled out bum first. (That made sure that Tom would say no more.)

Well even Mother asked me if I would like to take up this offer. Of course I refused. I guess mother felt that she had to ask me. I was not sure if she wanted to get rid of me or if she thought I would want to leave her because I was always with my father while Daisy and David were always with her and now that my father had gone would I feel unwanted. Anyway at that moment she was not herself. Now more than before I had to prove my worth but I did cry quietly each night for my loss was great. I got some paper and cut it into six pieces to make a diary. I had never had a diary but I knew the worth of one. I wanted to record these dates. I had two or three transfers including one of roses which I pressed on to the page containing the date of 9th January 1946 and wrote "roses for remembrance" I knew

I would never forget but the grief of a little girl of eleven losing her chief parent was all mine.

I was always with my father. I stayed at home with him he let me ride his bike I went to the market when he was selling or buying cows and stood at the ring with him (most times dying for a pee especially when I saw the cows doing just that as they went round the ring, there were no facilities for farmers never mind little girls at the market) while as usual Daisy and David went with Mother to town, shopping because Daisy was such a capable helper and David was the baby plus the aforesaid old adage of two is company, three's a crowd.

We all suffered a severe loss he was our father but he was also my pal. When strangers used to come to the house or farm when I was very young I always ran to my father in the same way as you all ran to your mother's leg of lap for security or comfort or to hide. There was no problem with my relationship with my mother but she had enough on her plate with a baby and Daisy to fend for. That's just how it was he was mine and I used to cuddle him, occasionally, whereas I do not remember mother being tactile with me or myself with her she was the old style Scottish mother, always there for you, always in the kitchen for you to return home to but no hug and no kiss. She was so predictable which is good for a child.

The burial on the 11the January 1946 was at Lesmahagow. We children did not go there. We stayed home and carried on with the work even David stayed with us this time.

The doctor who came to certify Father's death gave a new perspective on his illness. The pills prescribed by Doctor Arthur, he said, though they reduced or stopped the fits were only a palliative and damaged the heart. The haematoma in his head was continuing to grow and with medical knowledge at the stage it then was it was only a matter of time. The doctors paid by the insurance had lied in telling mother that he was cured and that same Dr. Arthur had been economical with the truth. Our family had been fobbed off with a pittance instead of being properly compensated for what was in fact a fatal industrial injury. All of this was now of course spilt milk and there was no use crying over it.

After a short and unsuccessful attempt to find a suitable dairyman to take father's place in running the business, the farm was put up for sale and was sold on the 2nd March 1946.

We all moved out and went to the Stewarts of Whinknowe Farm near Strathaven, Lanarkshire. They were relatives again and had three daughters. I believe Helen Stewart, the oldest daughter is still farming there to-day in 2004. The time at Whinknowe gave mother time to regroup her thoughts and her money. I remember she bought a baby seal fur coat. It was black and shiny and gorgeous. A real fur coat was a status symbol of wealth in the 30's and 40's. I felt that she was trying to hide some money so it was distributed amongst a few banks mostly savings type. At that time the government did not pry into your bank accounts as long as very little or no interest was appearing. The secret seemed to be to withdraw the interest as soon as it was about to be declared. So for a period of time I remember paying visits to banks frequently to lift the interest. Thus it would not be taxed. We all had some necessities and luxuries lavished on us at that time, like wrist watches each and two or three real silver bracelets each, again it was perhaps to conceal the huge profits of the previous year and prevent the Gordon Brown/chancellor of the day from appropriating our hard earned cash. The farm was sold for £2,350.00 I think. That was a lot of money in 1946.

But there were other sales plus the horses plus the cash that had not reached the bank plus the money in father's untouchable hoard. Mother was wealthy well at least seven thousand pounds in 1946 was a lot of money at a time when the widow's pension was 50 pence per week (it was called 10 shillings and there were 20 shillings in one pound and a widow was supposed to rear her family and pay her bills on that ½ of a pound coin alone weekly, there was no family allowance or tax credit or any other hand out from the government like you all and your mother received) so work that out for yourself,

Will that ever be folk?

a bungalow in the Glasgow Road in Paisley could be purchased for a little over £500 and would now in 2004 be bought for well over £800,000 pounds to more than millions.

This Whinknowe sojourn had to be seen to be believed. We had one big room the size of a ballroom so accommodation was good. We could use 1/3 as a furniture store, 1/3 as sitting area and 1/3 as sleeping areas. We had a bathroom and shared the large farm kitchen. The downside was the Stewart's love of cats. There must have been at least nine of these beasts and they seemed to live solely in the kitchen. I was easy to feed as I loved porridge and girdle or soda scones but when I saw these cats on the kitchen table where the baking had taken place I instantly became nauseated with any food from that kitchen. Mother tried her best to camouflage my refusal to eat by saying that Jane is just finicky. I quite like a cat even plural is al-right but as my personal food taster it was a negative. I had to live on bread out of the packet and milk and any food that we could buy to consume in our accommodation without cooking for example spam. I did not find that a problem so mother must have pandered to my whims.

However, after less than two months the usual solution was at hand, we were on the road again. For our next home mother purchased Croftfoot, Townhead Street, Strathaven. This was a beautiful semi- detached villa in a salubrious area. The other half of the villa was owned by a vet whose garden I used to weed diligently for which she gave me a ½ crown each time. (There were 8x ½ crowns in one pound so I was earning ¼ of the widow's weekly pension.) I gave it to mother with pride but it was a mere pittance.

This time the school was situated just over the wall from our walled garden which was great as we could have lengthy playtimes, no travelling and more time for our homework. I sat my eleven plus there and passed with an "A" thus I would now be in the top stream when I would go to secondary school. Surprisingly all these thirteen moves from school to school had not damaged the ability of all three of us to compete successfully in our examinations. Mother was very pleased with us all but she was starting to be quite restricting financially. I guess the purchase of the house and the need for elaborate carpeting and curtains and certain other essentials for the home plus our food, clothes, schooling and the realization that without the farm her children would require a proper education now that we were town people, let mother see how fast the money in the bank was going to slip away. (If we had remained as a farmer's daughters and son we would have been taken out of school as soon as possible to work on the farm and earn our keep. We would have gone to young farmer's dances and met and married a farmer and all lived happily ever after. That is how it was.)

But now mother wanted to make up the loss of a father to us and had calculated that without an income the few thousands in the bank would not last for the eight to ten years required to finish our educations properly. In the town there were expensive temptations and occupations like dancing classes, cinema visits, ice cream parlours, shopping, swimming lessons which if partaken of would unacceptably accelerate the drain on mother's fixed finances. Labour was the government in power. The country was on its knees after five debilitating years of war. Money in the bank was deflating. It did not take rocket science to realise that the government would find some use for her money so she had to invest it and find a solution for the present.

Our dog Ben was sold and Major (a Springer Spaniel) was bought on 10th June and as my birthday was on the 16th June I assumed he was my present from the family maybe not. We have a photo taken with Daisy, me and David and Major. The photo was taken in black and white or brown and white then at some later time mother had it coloureds professionally. It is a process quite unknown to-day except in old cinema productions. You could call it an antique. The only other place where I have seen this process carried out was on a photo of the Queen!! Yes that is true.

Will that ever be folk?

Mother was not afraid of work and would do anything to eke out a living but with three children under twelve she could not leave the home to go out to work. She must have answered some advert for a job as a housekeeper to a farmer in the highlands who was willing to take on a woman with child or children. Because the first I knew of it was the occasion when a visit to Rannoch was made by mother taking David with her as usual.

Within a month Croftfoot was sold on the 16th July 1946. After a few letters back and forth it was decided that John Mackenzie wanted to marry mother thus as his wife she would also be his house keeper. I think mother agreed unenthusiastically to the wedding but she did feel a tingle of the "tangle o' the isles" Sure by Tummel and Loch Rannoch and Loch Aber I will go seemed to star white highly in her vocal renditions from then on.

The proclamation of marriage was read on the 4th of August and the Wedding took place on the 9th of August in Braes of Rannoch Church. Mrs Outerson was the matron of honour and John Macdonald was best man. Now we had a stepfather and 2 stepsisters. One lived with her father in Camghouran Farm (Ivy is her name but she was called Yonnie)and the other Nelsis by name lived in Glenlyon with her grand parents and John Mackenzie's brother Dick who was unmarried and his sister Ina who was also a spinster. Daisy and I went to Rannoch by train on the 19th of August and Mum and David came up with the furniture from Strathavenon the 1st Sept 1946

Mother had sent Daisy and me on ahead so that we would be in place for the start of the new term at the Secondary School Breadalbane Academy, Aberfeldy by name. There was a delay for some unknown reason. I know mother was furious that we did not get into school at the beginning of the term thus she commenced her new life in Rannoch by having a good going verbal fight with Dojo's father Donald John Cameron Robertson of Dalreoch Farm who seemed to be the catalyst. I do not know who really was at fault but we missed ten or eleven essential weeks of secondary schooling at a very embryonic time in our education.

Camghouran Farm was a distance of twenty six miles of doubtful B class road from Aberfeldy. Our route to Aberfeldy was lengthened time and distance wise by the fact that we had to circumnavigate the whole loch (12 miles long) plus stop to pick up pupils at every farm or croft gate post. Buses were not as speedy and efficient as they are today so it took us about three hours for the aforementioned journey. As a result hostel accommodation was supplied for all pupils from Rannoch and Glenlyon. I believe the intake that August 1946 had been quite heavy plus very few if any pupils had left thus no place was available in the hostel for Daisy and me until after the Christmas Holidays. David was fine as he joined Yonnie at Dall Primary School just three miles down the road.

Thanks to mother's nagging we were squeezed in after the potato holidays, the 18th October 1946. Consequently from then till Christmas there was still no bed for us in the hostel so Daisy and I walked out at 10pm each night carrying our pyjamas and sponge bag and towel to go to sleep in a house up the road. Even in that house we did not have a bedroom we slept on the bed-settee in their sitting room. We slipped in very quietly; no one met us. We got into bed without a light, no hot water bottle and not only no kiss goodnight but also not even a word of welcome from the invisible owner (there was a street lamp outside).

In the morning we did the same quiet routine, quickly washed, dressed and made our way to the hostel for breakfast. We felt like orphan Annie, we had no table to study on in the study consequently no table drawer for our spare books, no bedroom in the hostel meant that we had no availability to a chest of drawers thus giving us no place to put our spare socks or pants or sponge bag and towel, and we could not leave anything in that sleeping-out accommodation as we did not even have a bedroom there.

Will that ever be folk?

I felt utterly unwanted and homeless. I have no idea what Daisy thought we did not speak about our inner feelings but I felt it was much harder for her. Although Daisy was always much bigger and more grown up than me I think she suffered more because the cosseting mother had given her meant she was not as able to suffer the slings and arrows of outrageous fortune as me. I felt there was a need for me to look out for her. However we were together at night but had to fight our own battles during the day and really like you two Hannah and Alice you want to be in with the crowd, be one of the set, making friends of your own, not stuck with only your sister.

To compound all this it was still 1946, the year in which our daddy had died, our mother had married again, we had a new home, a new step father and his daughter our new step sister who shared our bedroom at our new home Camghouran Farm. Further, both Daisy and I had missed about nine weeks of secondary school.

This was big, unlike at primary school we now had French, Latin, Geometry, Algebra, and for Daisy shorthand typing, Commercial Studies. We were ten weeks behind everyone in our class so in each lesson we had to try to do catch up plus keep ahead of the present daily class work. It was hard going. We must have been made of stern stuff. Withal I cannot remember being unhappy. We must have caught up with the class work because we progressed seamlessly from year to year Mother did a good job in the home front for us to remain so secure and confidant in ourselves although she never gave us praise or hugs or kisses. The old style Scottish mother was firm, strict, unsmiling but always there in the kitchen when you came home from school (in this present time we came home on Friday night at about 6pm. And left home for school on Monday morning at 6 am)

Mother now had four school children plus a husband and one or two shepherds for whom to launder, cook and clean with no electricity, no washing machine, no dishwasher, no Hoover, no fridge or deep freeze. Imagine Rebecca or Emma what life would be like with no T/V or DVD, ipod. or P.C. or i-phone. I had my piano and we had a wireless (you call it a radio) with a huge battery the size of the one in a car plus an accumulator which was filled with acid. This said accumulator had to be taken to the van (travelling shop) or to the village store to have the acid topped up with necessitous regularity. And woe betides the foolish girl who carried the accumulator carelessly as this would cause the acid to slop and thus burn into the skin or ruin the clothes of the bearer. There was no top or cap on the accumulator so these two aforementioned hazards did sometimes happen.

I can recall the varied daily routines and we as family had our duties to do in the home............... feed the hens, break up old crockery into little pieces for the hens to eat with their food to supply calcium so that their egg shells would be firm, feed the dogs (usually 3 or 4 collies) wash and dry the dishes, clean the lamps and globes, trim the wicks, fill the lamps and lanterns for the house and byre and out houses, wash and iron our clothes, thoroughly clean the house, pump up our bicycle tyres for our nights out at a whist and dance to which we would cycle 3 miles to Bridge of Gaur village hall (Braes of Rannoch sometimes called) and of course 3 miles home again at the end of the function which was usually 2 am. on a Friday or midnight on a Saturday. In amongst all this we had to find time to do our homework because we were expected to do well at school, failure was a non starter in the Watt or Jack regime. I digress to mention that we were never paid for work on the our farm nor did we ever expect payment like your father seems to have expected from Papa and I, his parents.

We all enjoyed helping Mother so these chores were not a punishment like you Emma or Alice or Hannah would have found them to be. We also did many things which you children to-day are forbidden to do alone, without parental supervision like playing in the burn, fishing for minnows of the trout or pike variety with our bare hands or a piece of string with a bent nail on one end and tied to a stick on the other end or swimming in the river, rafting on Loch

Rannoch with our rude pile of wood made into a raft and suspended in the loch shakily by dint of the empty sheep dip cans which we tied with bailing string to the bottom. (There was always a plentiful supply of this bailing string in the barn as it came off the bought in hay or was used for tying the stooks of corn). The raft and we always sank so not only did we have to hide the fact that we were soaked but we did not dare admit that we were almost drowned. No way could we run home crying like you always did as we would have been met with a further and more severe punishment from mother even if it was sometimes only her tongue. The trouble was that the maternal tonguing could last for days so it would have been better to have been given a good physical smacking and finish it now.

We spent the next day or so trying to get back into favour with mother and maybe even to make her smile as a bonus.

We took long walks in the hills summer and winter. In the summer we picked blaeberries, (in U.S.A they are called blue berries and in England they are bilberries) wild strawberries, hawthorn berries, raspberries and hazel nuts and ate them all as we were hungry like you Emma. We sat on the grass, sometimes it was an ant hill then we were covered in wee beasties which itched so we had to strip off and run like the wind to get rid of them or for speed we rolled down the hill and laughed and laughed hilariously at nothing in particular but it was fun. In the winter it was the snow and ice which afforded us the skating, sledging, hearing the stags baying for the rut, helping with the deer which was shot for our venison meals. Our homecoming was mixed with fear and trepidation in case our clothes, the red blotches on our bodies, our purple mouths and any other disfigurement was a give away. Or it may have been that our absence was noted because there was some undone duty. I guess the adrenalin flow of fear all added to the joy of life while experiencing these harmless, innocent and inexpensive pastimes.

In the winter as aforementioned the deer for our consumption was skinned, gutted and cut up most professionally into large pot size joints for pot roasting. As there was no fridge or freezer this meat was stored in the largest available receptacle namely the bath in the bathroom. Thus our bath was tied up for a month or so until another beast occupied it, could be another deer or a sheep for mutton. The bathroom was very cold anyway as we had no central heating nor were the windows double glazed but the preservation method used in the bath was not only the cold but also by dint covering the meat with coarse salt. Now our meals were great. I loved them. We had roast venison for dinner/high tea, cold venison for breakfast, stewed venison for lunch, boiled venison or fried venison or venison chops for a change until it was all done!.

To this day my favourite roasts are venison and lamb or mutton so obviously I had no objection to the monotony of the menu or the fact that the bath was occupied for a few weeks while these meats got pride of place. As the bathroom was a big room on the ground floor and near the only door it was quite multi purpose. We sometimes parked our bicycles, plus the hundred weight bags of hen meal and dog flake meal in there too. This afforded a storage place both dry and convenient for speedy use.

Daisy and I were at the hostel all week where we could bath and wash our hair like all the other girls at least once or twice per week by a rota system.

By 1948 David and Yonnie (Ivy Mackenzie our step sister) had joined us at school in Breadalbane Academy, Aberfeldy. They too were in the hostel, Dunollie House for the girls and Craigthuil House for the boys.

Big people did not bath frequently as they do now. In fact some adults would go through their whole life without ever bathing. The most popular washing place for the men folk was the large 'wally' kitchen or scullery sink or the large water tub outside or the horse trough where they would strip to the waist in all weathers and wash down as far as possible and sometimes even wash 'possible'. There was also the availability of swimming in the burn or the loch on a hot day. (I did that often, in fact I took my first tentative whole body immersion in the Camghouran Burn with the floatation aid of an R.A.F reject belt which I had bought through an advert in the Scottish Farmer.)

The most important part of the body, the feet, were always well cared for, for example after a long day out on the hill in all weathers one often soaked them in a hot mustard bath by the fireside after having stripped off, had a good rub down with a rough towel to boost the circulation and changed into warm dry clothes. Sheer bliss!! (This addition of mustard to the water in the foot bath or basin was a cure for all ailments particularly a head cold or in fact any chill. Nowadays you would simply have a warm bath as all your rooms are heated, you have electricity and constant hot running water and of course you take it all for granted.) In the summer the whole house was warm but in the winter every room except the kitchen/living room was frozen. In fact the frost was inside the window as well as outside the window most mornings. We dressed like greased lightening as soon as we had crawled out of our warm bed. I can tell you it certainly was not a life for wimps but as explained we were very comfortable and perhaps more happy than you or many of the children to-day. Strangely I do not remember ever feeling cold inside or outside the house.

Mother bought a New Hudson two stroke motor bike for Daisy. It was like a thick cycle with an engine (not like a moped) and could travel at 40 miles per hour flat out once you got it kick started. I have no idea why this purchase was made unless it was for us to use to go the dances instead of bikes. Whatever the reason it was very useful for me during the summer between my 5th and 6th year at Breadalbane Academy because I took a job as assistant cook alias dogs body at Fortingal Hotel outside Aberfeldy on the Rannoch side, at the mouth of the road to Glenlyon. I was paid the handsome sum of £2 per week for my slavery there where I worked from 5am to 11pm seven days per week for a period of 6 weeks. My means of transport was the New Hudson 2 stroke and one day per week I shot up home to Camghouran to see mother arriving at midnight and leaving at 2am. On reflection perhaps I kept her out of bed I did not stop the think other than that she would be delighted to see me. My visits would have been of a surprise nature as we had no phone, no mobile, no fax, no P.C. Children are a selfish self centred species particularly to their parents.

I sometimes went to dance to Jim Cameron country dance band at Killin using the 2 stroke. It was quite scary and eerie toot ling along these lonely roads on my own always late at night with no protection from marauders. I remember one night as I was making my way home to Fortingal from the Killin Dance Hall at 2/3 am I beheld two or three men in a state of inebriation weaving their way up the hill on the side of Loch Tay along the road I had to travel. I knew they would hear the putt putt of my engine and look round so my only escape was to open throttle, gather momentum at the bottom of the hill and aim to fly past them at full forty miles. Such was not to be; my wee engine would do only 20 mph up hill which was almost running pace. I was scared stiff as the men were spread across the road and I had to cut through them. One of them put his hand out to catch me and did in fact touch my coat. I felt like Tam o' Shanter's grey mare and was ready to discard the wretched garment while concentrating on making the final lurch to reach the top of the hill where safety would rein since I knew the engine would leap to 40 mph. on the flat (in the grey mare's case it was her tail she lost to the witches and warlocks). See Tam o' Shanter.

One did not have fears of meeting dangerous people on lonely roads in the 1940 and 1950's although there was always a need for caution and being on risk assessment alert. Throughout the north of the highlands there were Hydro Electric Works in progress building dams et etcetera to make electricity from high speed waterfalls. For these works men were imported from Ireland and other parts of Scotland and they were wrongly collectively called navvies. They were mostly nice people but locals always felt a hint of danger when a crowd of male incomers were herded together.

Our life at Rannoch was passing most happily. We were all in a routine of school during the week and home to the farm at the weekends. But as usual that was about to change. Mother was not happy. She never discussed her problems with me. I feel she may have confided in Daisy but the subject was not mentioned. I found out only when we were up sticks and leaving to go to a far place. I asked if I could stay at school in Aberfeldy till the end of that term/year and live in the hostel by myself at the weekends so that I could sit my final year exams.

The Education Authorities permitted me to do that so Daisy, David and Mother all went to West Linton in Peeblesshire in 1948 with our furniture, such as was left of that which we had brought with us to Camghouran Farm in 1946. Mother was not well, her whole system had poisoned and she had jaundice amongst other things. There were reasons. She had fallen pregnant with John Mackenzie (her husband) and she did not want the complication or bond of another child. The child was either aborted or she conveniently lost it and Daisy was kept off school to help mother through her ensuing illness. She needed a change or a long holiday and that was how she operated. I knew nothing of this at the time as David and I were at school. The brunt of mother's problems always fell on Daisy's young shoulders. Daisy was a big girl compared to me so she seemed much older. Remember there were only fifteen months between Daisy and me. (I was the build of Becky even when I was 15.)

Also Mackenzie was hassling mother for her money. He perhaps thought it was his right to get the use of the wealth of this rich widow whom he had married. Perhaps he felt that he could expand his sheep stock or pay some debts or such. Anyway it was a no go area. Mother was determined to keep this money for herself and more importantly for David Watt's children viz a viz Daisy, Jane and David Watt and no one else. She knew that our father had skimped and saved all his life, had worked punishing hours every day of the week, did not know the words holiday or time off so she was the custodian of this money and had no intention of spending it unwisely. She had gone to Rannoch to save Dad's money for us and she left for the same reason.

This time we stayed in a farm cottage of Halmyre Mains Farm, West Linton and mother and Daisy worked in the dairy there. So now we had a tied house, free potatoes, milk and coal, an income and mother's money so we were financially sound. Mother, who loved to get to town to shop, could get the 'bus to Edinburgh and our life now became a round of outings to the cinema, the zoo, concerts, Sunday school, church, youth fellowship and various other whist drives and dances for Daisy and me.

Daisy and I had a great social life mostly hinging around the church ancillaries. Myself and two boys from the Heriot-Watt College in Edinburgh were the Sunday School teachers and I played the piano for the singing of the hymns for my Sunday School. I also played the huge organ in the church on Sundays for our minister Rev. T. Hall. I had no tuition on organ playing so I just treated it like a piano then pulled out as many stops as I thought to be necessary and made a great base and tenor sound. It went down well and no one knew how ignorant I was. I was nervous of course.

After the summer holidays Daisy and I went to the High School in Peebles. We travelled by 'bus daily so we were home each night for a change. Mother bought me a piano and paid for piano lessons for me with a music teacher in West Linton once a week until he told me he could not take me any further as I now knew all he was capable of teaching me.

Daisy had lessons on the violin and mother gave her own violin to Daisy and bought her a leather music case. We all seemed happy there. David went to West Linton primary school. I remember the school work was hard for me at the beginning of the term in my new school Peebles High School. Daisy must have met a similar problem. The books were all more advanced than those we had used at Breadalbane Academy, for me that was Latin, French, Maths, Arithmetic, History, English and even Geography, Art and Music. So now apart from having to keep abreast with the homework of all these subjects daily I had to do catch up as I was so far behind my classmates.

A super wee rich girl Libby Rankine befriended me and gave me her old jotters to take home so that I could copy the back work into mine and learn it. She helped me during break times and lunch times at school as I went home by 'bus each night she and I had to do all that work during the day which was fantastic for me and so kind of her. When I had caught up we still spent our free school time together at her house (which was just over the school wall) with her spaniel puppies. I think her mother was a closet breeder. (a hobby) Other times Libby taught me the Highland fling and various other highland and Scottish country dance steps.

Libby went to dance lessons almost every night in Peebles as she lived in the town and not only was her father still alive but he was quite wealthy. She was a beautiful, accomplished dancer and the correct size and shape for ballet. With her help and guidance plus the dancing we learned at the youth fellowship club Daisy and I were good enough to dance on the stage at the fund-raising concerts in the village hall although neither of us had ever had a formal dancing lesson in our lives. (This is not true. I went to tap dancing classes for two weeks, only, in Strathaven in 1946. Mother put an abrupt stop to them when I came home asking for tap shoes and a tutu or something similar to wear as a dancing dress. She sussed instantly that this would be an ongoing unnecessary expense. Money was not for wasting on frivolities as our father was dead and mother was dipping heavily into her inheritance with no means of replenishment in sight.)

[As an aside I shall say now I lost touch with Libby for fifty years but managed to track her down through her brother when I was in Stobo Castle Health Spa near Peebles in 1989. Libby was in

Australia, was a born again Christian, a dance teacher, (would you believe) a mother and grandmother. In the year 2000, fifty two years after I had last seen Libby, she and her husband Len came to stay with us at Greshornish House for a week and I took them plus your great Aunt Cathy (MacPhie/Macfarland) and you Hannah to the Three Chimney's Restaurant for lunch and Hannah at just 2 years old behaved like a little lady. We still keep in touch with Libby at Christmas and B.M. your 'Uncie' visited Libby and Len when he was in Australia in 1996.] As an addendum I shall say Libby died of cancer in 2009.

While at Peebles High School I also had swimming, tennis and net ball lessons and I was in the net ball team; whereas at Breadalbane Academy our sports were rounders, gymnastics and hockey. I was always in the first X1 hockey. In fact I loved hockey so much (sort of like shinty) that I wanted to form a ladies hockey team later in life but I never quite found the time as I was too busy studying.

Our sojourn to Peeblesshire lasted almost a year and then we found ourselves back in Rannoch. I was not informed of the reason for the return but if there was any permanence in our home abode it seemed to be Camghouran Farm and I guess mother's health had improved sufficiently for her to be able to cope with the boring grind of her life there. We self centred, selfish children were unaware of her misery because we enjoyed our life in Rannoch and Aberfeldy so much. My school work was easy for the first term as I was now ahead of Breadalbane and my country dancing also took an upturn, thanks to Libby' tuition I was chosen to represent Scotland. I was picked along with 47 other girls to represent Scotland to dance in a sixteen some reel surrounded by four eight some reels in the Royal Albert Hall in London in November 1949 in front of Royalty. The occasion was a Red Cross Anniversary. (I think 25th) and we were all in the Red Cross or Junior Red Cross.

That is why every time I see the Royal Albert Hall being featured on T/V I say I danced there. It was a great honour and my feet

Will that ever be folk?

worked hard to be chosen. Ever after that in the dance hall at Braes of Rannoch I was aware that my footwork was being closely inspected while I danced the set dances there. (Quadrilles, Lancers, Reel of the 51st, La Russe, not forgetting the ubiquitous eight some reel and many many more as we did and naturally in a show off way being a bit proud of my skill I pandered to my audience by making my steps more perfect for them to inspect.

Now Daisy and I were in the full swing of ceilidhs and dances, whist drives and dances, boyfriends and the full enjoyment of our simple, innocent pleasures in the company of boyfriends. Daisy had three faithful swains from which to choose. My favourite for her was John MacDonald. He was gorgeous. He was tall and fair and handsome and a game keeper same as his father. All the game keepers were tall and handsome and they wore these plus four tweed trousers, both at work and when dressed and boy were they stately. After all Queen Victoria fell for her gamekeeper!!.

These highland gamekeepers not only had stature and a certain presence acquired through rubbing shoulders with royalty and nobility but were also so damned handsome. John's mother and father were so super with us too. But Daisy was too young in herself and just said much later that she was not ready for marriage so when we eventually moved away from Rannoch as I shall explain later she did not keep in touch, she was too high and mighty and the opportunity passed. John was a Catholic but so what. I think that may have been important at the time. Mother would not have approved and we all tried to please mother as best we could. In mother's book any marriage was a non starter so we should have pleased ourselves while we had the chance but unlike you six we were not allowed to become too intimate with any boy. Dancing was acceptable but no more than that was a no no.

Daisy and I joined the Church of Scotland at the Braes of Rannoch Parish Church. We cycled there on Sundays and for the last 2 years there I played the organ. I felt sure there were more proficient organists than me but no one else offered at that time. I pulled out all the stops on that organ too and had the added task of having to peddle furiously to blow up the bellows I suppose. It was hard work and quite nerve racking.

For my part my boyfriend of three long lovely years was David Mac Martin. He was also a gamekeeper's son. He was O K. (not as handsome as John) but he and I were friends at school together and at the Braes of Rannoch dances, ceilidhs and whist drives. He was in the year below me so when I left to go to college in Glasgow he was still in Aberfeldy for a further year and all the girls who found him attractive could get an innings now that I had gone. He was my faithful boyfriend from 1949 to 1952. In the words of the song 'Roses are red my love' we did in fact date through High School!!

When I left Rannoch to go to college mother came too and eventually bought a flat in Denny so that I could commute from there to Glasgow. Actually our flitting and furniture leaving Camghouran was done by a cattle float belonging to the farmer at Castlecary where mother and I were engaged for dairy work and into whose farm cottage we set up home. (tied house again). That was mother's clever ruse to enable her to make her escape from Rannoch for good and get her flitting free and be supplied with a house for free as a stop gap till she could look around and buy a house of her own. Well remember there was no internet, no phone, no fax and nor even a pigeon.

It was good. I got up at 5am to help mother for two or three hours before going home to wash and dress to go to The Glasgow west of Scotland College of Domestic Science (Do. School for short) for a w and W 10 am start five or six days a week. My course was the I.M.A. (Institutional Management Association degree). All the girls in my class there were most posh and townie and to compound my feelings of 'fish our of water' and 'a country bumpkin' my heart was breaking from loss of Rannoch and that whole life style plus of course the boy I left behind me.

When I came home at night I helped mother again from 5-7pm. I was not as good as Daisy at this work but I did my best and thought I was great. I think the farmer was disappointed maybe even annoyed that he got me instead of Daisy as he had met her in Camghouran when he came to interview mother. I suppose he assumed 'the daughter' mentioned in the contract would be Daisy and mother did not elaborate or clarify. I did my best and in a twisted sort of way quite enjoyed the byre and dairy twice daily routine enlightened by the presence of not one but two fifteen year old boys (I was eighteen) armed with typical Glaswegian humour who had a sort of crush on me which manifested itself by bombarding me with their constant clever and entertaining banter when I was on duty with mother. This caused me to have great difficulty stifling my mirth in case of the words of the song don't laugh at my jokes too much; people will say w'ere in love would be interpreted.

The only downside was that as winter was coming in my hands were rough, red and work worn with the constant exposure to cold water. Then I had to run like the wind to catch my bus at the top of the hill (almost a mile) and arrive in College looking a wreck. One is conscious of one's appearance when one is surrounded by and mixing with these posh little ladies which the Do. School spawned who perhaps yawned and stretched at 9.am, dressed carefully, applied their make up expertly and teetered out on their stilettos to Daddy's waiting Jaguar, arrived with every strand of hair in place while serenading us in the cloakroom with the strains of Walking my baby back home. (this was number one hit song by Jimmy Young that year 1952).

I was an outsider, far from home with no boyfriend and no social life in the beginning and felt that I would never blend in here. But once we had donned our overalls and caps (green for sewing and dressmaking, blue for Laundry and sciences and English and Electricity, White for cookery and catering subjects) removed all make up and jewelry, (house rules) we all looked financially the same so the snobbery would now be judged by the brain power and there I knew I would shine or make bloody sure that I did.

I got a substantial bursary/grant for my studies and I bought a cycle with some of the money. Mother had her own cycle which she had kept good all these years. It was a Raleigh Racer with the low curling handle bars.

Mother applied to adverts for houses and flats for sale and we cycled around Stirlingshire some nights after work in order to check out those which seemed to be suitable. Eventually we settled for 6a East Borland Place, Denny and left the farm to settle in Denny. I had no problem with my studies and applied myself diligently because I knew I had to succeed as mother had gone to a lot of trouble to accommodate my career. Mother never complained but Daisy did.

I was trying hard to ignore by broken heart at leaving Rannoch, and had almost succeeded when my faithful swain sent me a 'Dear John' letter. That was the cruellest cut. It took me a long time to surface from that blow. It was so brutal when one was so down in spirit and in a strange land with strange people. Mother said nothing but she must have noticed.

David and Daisy stayed on at Camghouran for a few weeks to help John Mackenzie then they joined us in Denny. David went to Denny High School for a year before he did Advanced Maths and Dynamics and 'golf' at Stirling High School for a further year as he was too young to go to University although his entrance had been accepted at sixteen. Then he went to Glasgow University to do Honours Geology Degree from where he graduated first class in the fullness of time. He was also Senior Sports Champion at Aberfeldy and Denny and the talent scouts were forcefully pursuing him. Mother intercepted again and insisted that there was no future in a sport, What happens when you are a 'has been' No, you must get your education first.

Daisy went to Auchencruive Agricultural College, Ayrshire to do dairying, agriculture and milk recording. She passed out of that

successfully and as there was no farm of her own in sight she settled for doing milk recording. I do not think mother was too keen for her to continue that lark as it meant living out of a suitcase like Kate Adie and accepting the second rate accommodation offered to the milk recorder by the mostly mean farmers also the pay did not justify the discomfort and inconvenience of moving daily from farm to farm without a car.

Mother rescued her again and a post as sub-postmistress at Crianlarich loomed on the horizon. Daisy seemed to enjoy that. Aunt Annie, Uncle Jock and I visited her there to brighten up her social life. I think she had a faithful swain, a farmer's son from the nearest farm to Crianlarich Village on the south side going towards Callendar so perhaps our efforts were surplus to requirements. This fellow, Ian, had red hair that I know but I do not remember his surname. Perhaps his grandson is at present there.

Marjory Lochhead and I hitch hiked from Denny to Crianlarich to see Daisy and we took Bed and Breakfast in a Youth Hostel. We had joined the Youth Hostel Association earlier thus we could hitch or hike between hostels on our way up north and south again to Denny. It was a great holiday for Marjory and I. We even included Aberfeldy, the Black Watch Monument, the villages Weem, Fortingall and part of Glenlyon.

While I was in Denny not only did I work seriously and diligently at my studies in college but I also took outside examinations which were optional and for which I had to attend college on Saturdays. (Having a weekly or monthly season ticket for the bus travel it meant the Saturday journey from Denny to Glasgow was not an additional expense). My first thought always was can I afford to do this? Mother had said that the money she had saved from her legacy would be enough to see all of us through to a good education but then the tap would dry up so I tried to do my best to lengthen the financial allowance time. Being economical was no hardship to me as that quality was inbred. The waste one sees today is destroying the planet but few care. I do not suppose any of you ever thought 'can my parents afford this?'

Life was not all work and no play during these two years in Denny. David and I went ice skating in the Falkirk Ice Rink some Saturday afternoons; I went dancing in the Stirling Plaza or Doaks's in Falkirk with Marjorie or Helen Boyd. I knew all the girls in the Denny Land Rangers by now as I had joined that association quite early on. The Land Rangers and the Sea Rangers are both a continuation of the Guiding movement. You pass from Rainbow, to Brownies to Guides to Rangers. You can join one of these Rangers from 16 to 21 year old.

I went on holiday for a fortnight to France and Switzerland with fourteen of the Land Rangers in 1952. Added to these activities I played Badminton in the Denny Parish Church hall with some of the youth fellowship and acquired the friendship of Willie Mackintosh there. He and I played tennis frequently and he sometimes took me to the cinema. In Do. School I had by now a particular friend Sheen Webster. We had been thrown together alphabetically. (Watt and Webster). Fortunately we complemented each other almost instantly. I thought Sheena was beautiful but a bit prim so I had to work on her to get her to do some risky deeds like dodging home at 3pm when our assignment was finished instead of waiting till 4pm. She lived in Falkirk so we were rushing to the same bus station. We even went to the University Union Dances on Saturday night and rushed out together for our last buses at 11pm; doing a sort of Cinderella act.

By now Sheena and I had joined up with another two girls at Do School; they were Joyce Mackie and Margaret Letham both from Kilmarnock so now we had formed a formidable foursome. I felt totally integrated and at home with them and we used to go out to Kelvin Grove Park on sunny summer days at lunch time and sometimes accidentally or intentionally met three boys from the University. All of these people star in my photograph album. Sheena and Joyce have kept in touch all these years and have come to visit me at Greshornish in the 1980's. Apart from all that the journeys to and fro from Denny to Glasgow by bus afforded the opportunity to meet certain other passengers with a calculated regularity. One could say another boy meets girl occasion. The buses at the times between 8.am and 8.30am from Denny Cross had come from Stirling and were well used by Glasgow University students, Jordanhill Teacher's College students, Glasgow Vet College students and Do School students which meant fun time for the making of new friends and meeting up with acquaintance which all added to the variety of conversations and sometimes even dates.

I obtained my I.M.A. diploma in 1954 and left all this behind to go to Radbrook College in Shrewsbury (Shropshire). I could have gone to Stirling Infirmary and travelled daily but for some vague reason I decided to leave home. David was with Mother so she was O.K. and Daisy was there sometimes too. Maybe I felt that as I was not leaving mother by herself I should spread my wings. The College gave us addresses of acceptable placements as we were still under their umbrella for a further year. During this time we had to write a thesis (My thesis was Modern Methods of Processing and Preserving Food) and give a description of our duties and the equipment we used plus of course we had a job/post and we were paid for our work plus given free accommodation and food and one day off each week.

Having chosen Radbrook College and having gone for an interview, for which I was paid, and having been accepted I had burned my boats so now had to work there for a year at least then come back to Glasgow Do School for my oral examination and thesis criticism plus a few other hassles. If I left within the year all my last two years were a failure although I had passed my college examinations with flying colours.

All this college stuff I allude to is actually University in the 21st Century. One seldom talks about college. All these further education outlets are University! In fact I believe one graduates from kindergarten now with a good degree in alphabetical qualifications and it is always a first!

When I arrived in Radbrook in September 1954 I found myself painfully homesick again. What had I done? I should have accepted the post in Stirling Infirmary? There was no need for me to put myself through all this ongoing heartbreak. Surely, Jane you could have seen this coming. Well here I am and I must stick it out come what may. I bought the Sunday Post and yearned for the Scottish loaf and was longing to see anything Scottish. Here I was alone in deep England bordering Wales (in fact Shrewsbury has a Welsh Bridge and an English bridge) where everyone spoke English and were so poshly spoken and most upmarket.

I hated it all. Added to my misery was the fact that Miss Lindop our head caterer, thus immediate boss, disliked me. Well she would have disliked anyone who had taken this post as the girl I replaced (Miss Williams) was her special favourite blue eyed girl whom she loved dearly. On reflection from a distance of 50years I feel that there may even have been a lesbian like attraction between Miss Lindop and Miss Williams (Miss Williams is still unmarried). Miss Lindop picked on me almost every day for no real reason. If I could have left I would have I was so miserable. The other girls were good with me but that woman was the pits. She had migraine headaches quite often and when I saw her approach the kitchen with the gray scowl in place I knew I was in for it in some way so braced myself for the onslaught. I was good at my work and not only was it easy for me but also I knew I was highly proficient in every way and well on top of the job. One small example I shall bore you with but I could tell you them all as you know in life you remember all the good times and you remember all the bad time but you forget the mediocre times. This is it.

Radbrook College taught students for cookery, housekeeping, dairy work, poultry work, gardening and the I.M.A. and Teachers of Home Economics. As most of the students were resident in college their culinary efforts were brought to us in the catering kitchen. We had to incorporate these messy indiscriminate individual little dishes of fish pie or rice pudding or steak pie or eve's pudding et etcetera into our menu for the lunch or dinner for the students that day or that night or the next day so if we were doing roast beef or roast lamb or roast pork or whatever for the students lunch we would calculate how many portions we would get from our student's efforts and add or subtract from our roast beef or whatever we were offering that day. So I would calculate 45 portions of fish pie, 50 portions of fish turnovers, and as the full complement of the college number was say 150 students I would need 55 portions of roast beef from our kitchen. But just in case I would always leave a slack of 10-20 portions thus go for 70 to 75 portions of roast beef. I knew I was good at catering and stood with confidence behind the service hatch as the students passed through choosing what dish they preferred. The first come first serve rule applied and after that the last lot got what was left but usually there was no problem because the students wanted to sample it all and particularly their own food.

I would be all polished and prepared and the gong would ring for the students to mill through to collect their lunch from the hatch where we kitchen staff were all standing to attention and serving the food to the students. Lo and behold at this point up would crawl Miss Lindop, position her fat distended stomach behind me and say loudly in my ear do you think you look all right? I thought she meant that my overall was dirty so I looked at it to ascertain the picture and said yes. I don't know how you can stand there.!! She just stood there throughout the whole service of the meal then at the end when all was well and pretty damned neat as to portion calculation, very little left over if any, perfect catering one could say she said "the devil looks after his own" No thanks for my good job or neat calculations.

That was how she treated me for a whole year. It was bloody awful. A lesser person would have shrivelled into a snivelling wreck. Here I was a twenty year old Scottish girl from the wilds of Rannoch all alone and heartbroken in a strange country. But thanks to my back bone and the fact that Miss Davie who took her first class honours degree at Marishall College, Aberdeen and who taught us Latin in Breadalbane Academy, Aberfeldy said 'girls, now you are equipped to speak to the King or the Prime Minister' as I had the audacity to believe her words no one was going to destroy me as a result of lack of knowledge or competence in my chosen subject. Miss Davie said I was capable.

As assistant cook I was paid £12 per month. Actually I did not need any money as all my necessities were there in the accommodation and my going out was mostly paid for me by my boy friends who materialized once I had settled in and found some contacts via Gill and Dorothy.

I did not buy any clothes as I had plenty already and I was never a 'slave to fashion'. Remember also it was 1952 and some rationing still existed. At work we wore only our underwear covered by a white overall and cap all laundered for us so no clothes were required, no petrol and no travelling expenses. That mere pittance of money was ample for me. In fact I could afford to send money home and take driving lessons. I passed my test in Shrewsbury. (£8 for 10 lessons. I had 22 lessons then paid for my test so it probably cost me £23, two month's wages)

To cut a long story short I integrated well and found my feet and held my head high and was perhaps not only accepted but also an asset in the quest for boyfriends for Gill and Dorothy. Miss Lindop was rather surprised and questioned what attracted the English Public School boys to me. She concluded that it was my red hair and Scottish accent. Actually it was the fact that by dint of a co-ed education and a brother who kept on bringing his pals home for me to look after and feed et etcetera plus my Denny days, my Rannoch days and hostel days all with an equal mix of male and female presence I was quite unfazed by male company. They were just people to me, whereas to Dorothy and Gill, and the other boarding school educated girls, boys were an unknown species whose presence was quite daunting, thus creating a certain coyness and shyness in their demeanour which meant that I became unwittingly a sort of ice breaker.

My 21st birthday was in June 1955 and Miss Lindop excelled there. The whole catering staff led by Miss Lindop laid on a great party for me, food, cake, candles and beautiful, expensive presents from every one of them e.g. bedside lamp, leather writing case, leather suitcase, brief case, travelling alarm clock et etcetera. I had never before had such a display of party food and beautiful presents all at the one time for just me. It was wonderful. I was in a state of shock. Now I knew that not only had I been accepted by my peers but also by Miss Lindop. From then on I felt almost at home in Shrewsbury and could almost have lived there. The big word was almost. I was not ready to break the ties of home and home was always where mother was and whenever an opportunity arose I went home to Mother in Denny.

Gill and Dorothy and Mary Williams were going to Jersey on holiday that summer and asked me to join them. I refused as I felt it would be mean of me to go away to enjoy myself and spend money unnecessarily without mother being there. Also I did so want to go home. I was only 21 years old and very young for my age. In Denny mother and I had been like sisters for a short time at least. We had gone to the cinema and gone out cycling together and I think mother was happy there.

I travelled to and from Denny by train. I left Shrewsbury at 9pm and arrived in Crewe at 11pm. I got off the train in Crewe and waited there for 2 or 3 hours for the express train from London to North of Scotland which passed through Crewe. (If you ever see the film A Brief Encounter by David Leam you will see there the type of tearoom and rest room in which I spent these three lonely, cold, miserable hours.) The train trundled through the night and although it had no refreshment room or dining room on board (very basic facilities) you were allowed time to leave the compartment at one or two designated stations en route to get a mug of tea. On my journeys north for the Christmas break my travelling companions at that time of night were mostly servicemen in uniform from Aldershot or such I presume. They were most kind and kept me plied with tea and food at these stops. In 1955 one did not think that there was malice abroad. At least it never entered my head. At no time during these long over night journeys did I feel threatened by dint of travelling in a railway carriage with eight or ten servicemen. I even slept.

I got off at Stirling and walked to the bus station to get the Glasgow bus which passed through Denny. Got off at Denny Cross and walked down Broad Street arriving home at 8am a mere eleven hours after leaving Radbrook. I think mother was pleased to see me. It was difficult to tell as she was never tactile. Hugging and kissing was not a normal greeting with the general run of Scottish mothers but somehow mother did instil in one a knowledge that not only did she have your best interests at heart in her inimitable fashion but also that she would always be there for you. I guess that is why I went home. Since my father's death in 1946 her sole aim had been to see the three of us educated, grown up, honest and successful.

Mother had no hobbies, no husband, and at that time there was no t/v or DVD etc. so we were her entire life. She did read books in fact it was she who introduced me to Dickens, Jane Austen, the Bronte Sisters and Rebecca, Wuthering Heights and Jane Eyre to mention just a handful. I still had some friends in Denny and perhaps a faithful or maybe unfaithful swain or two. If the swains were unfaithful it was no sweat as my heart had been broken and patched enough so that now I had casual male friends. Willie Mackintosh was still around and keen to see me!!

Gill, Dorothy and I went out quite a lot together. One particular night I shall mention in detail as that was the night Gill met her husband to be. We went to the Young Farmers Dance in the Lion Hotel. It was Gill who instigated this outing. We were all decked out in long evening dresses as one did in these days for a special occasion so we hired a taxi to make a stylish arrival but as funds were being stretched to the outer limits we made a pact that the first one of us to get the offer of a lift home to Radbrook would insist on her other two friends being included in the transport thus we would not have the expense of a taxi for the return journey at that time in the morning.

We attracted three fellows, two of them with their own farm and one who was a farm manager. Mike, Jack and Gerald were their names. Mike never looked at a girl as he was too shy but he took an instant fancy to me and the other two noticed us simultaneously. Our destiny was sealed thanks to Mike. The other two conveniently held back to let Mike get a clear run so that meant Jack asked Gill and Gerald took Dorothy to dance. Gill told us, early on, that she had a lift home with Jack. I said 'good' and could now enjoy the dance in the knowledge that I could be free to go home without an attachment. Mike did ask me to take a lift with him but I had already said yes to Gill and did not wish to rock the boat. The out come was that Gill, Dorothy and I all crushed up together on the front of Jacks smelly old land rover with a bench seat and operated by a gear stick on the steering wheel. (All these facilities are illegal by to-day's regulations but quite O.K. in the 1950's). Mike drove home alone in his flashy maroon coloured Humber Super Snipe with chrome wheels that night. I still did not fancy him although he was very nice. I could not be bought by his luxurious limousine. He did visit Radbrook to see me and I did go out with him because I felt it would be churlish of me to refuse and spoil the foursome or six some which was evolving. We made quite a formidable crowd and it was good fun.

I noted very soon that Mike had had his car seats upholstered in tartan especially for this Scottish girl. Eventually Jack and Gill got engaged to be married and their wedding day was set for January 1956 so of course Gill gave in her notice to leave in August 1955. As my compulsory year was at an end in August 1955 and I had been back to Do. School for my final Criticism Examination plus Oral Examination plus the marking of my thesis all of which I had passed with flying colours I gave in my notice to leave Radbrook College by Christmas 1955.

to hell or to heaven. The all important necessity was to prevent a disgrace from being thrust upon the family. We had not only the stigma of producing a bastard child but also the unforgivable disgrace of a divorce hanging like the sword of Damocles over our head forcing us to keep ourselves decent. I feel it was a pity that we did not have the opportunities of the full 'Monty' like you have today because many girls found out too late and to their chagrin that the da Meanwhile I was gathering boyfriends like 'rosebuds while you may' and life was fantastic. I was on a roller. I had Harper Adams Agricultural College students eating out of my hands. Why I do not know because unlike most of the girls do to-day I did not have sex or anywhere near it with any of these boys so none of them got their wicked way with me. I did not know the word 'condom' and we had no pills to prevent us from becoming pregnant. If I had conceived a child out of wedlock I would have had to commit suicide like most of the decent girls did way back then. Mother would have thrown me out well that is what I thought and the thought was enough to make me not only keep all my clothes on but also in the words of the prophet 'keep my legs crossed' We went dancing or to the cinema or out for a run in our escort's car. We held hands and kissed and cuddled and felt most excited as to what it would be like to take all these rousing feelings a few stages further. The thrill of wondering was as close as it got to the expectation of the ecstasy awaiting our joy of the uninhibited, legal penetration of the sex act in a loving marriage. In most cases it was a tumultuous disappointment. I am led to believe that some times it was a great disappointment.

What could one do? 'You have made your bed so you can lie on it' was the sermon from the Scottish Presbyterian mother which formed a lasting cementing of her daughter's marriage, be it to hell or to heaven. The all important necessity was to prevent a disgrace from being thrust upon the family. We had not only the stigma of producing a bastard child but also the unforgivable disgrace of a divorce hanging like the sword of Damocles over our head forcing us to keep ourselves decent. I feel it was a pity that we did not have the opportunities of the full 'Monty' like you have today because many girls found out too late and to their chagrin that the daMeanwhile I was gathering boyfriends like erosebuds while you may f and life was fantastic. I was on a roller. I had Harper Adams Agricultural College students eating out of my hands. Why I do not know because unlike most of the girls do to-day I did not have sex or anywhere near it with any of these boys so none of them got their wicked way with me. I did not know the word econdom f and we had no pills to prevent us from becoming pregnant. If I had conceived a child out of wedlock I would have had to commit suicide like most of the decent girls did way back then. Mother would have thrown me out well that is what I thought and the thought was enough to make me not only keep all my clothes on but also in the words of the prophet keep my legs crossed. We went dancing or to the cinema or out for a run in our escort car. We held hands and kissed and cuddled and felt most excited as to what it would be like to take all these rousing feelings a few stages further. The thrill of wondering was as close as it got to the expectation of the ecstasy awaiting our joy of the uninhibited, legal penetration of the sex act in a loving marriage. In most cases it was a tumultuous disappointment.

Finding the fellow they had married was not all that he had portended to be in his performance in the boudoir. There was no Viagra. There were no sex toys. There was no mention to be made of what went on inside the bedroom before marriage so we all went there like lambs to the slaughter in ignorance, lack of know how and entering the domain of the unmentioned deed with no escape available. It was still a man's world which meant men were all powerful in every way. Woe betides the new raw wife who would be bold enough to mention that perhaps the performance in bed was not her fault. Everything that went wrong in the marital bed or any lack of or poor performance on the husband's part was blamed on the new young wife.

There was no t/v and no pornographic films and no exposure of two people copulating in the most graphic and explanatory way complete with the sound effect of the grunting and squealing like you see portrayed in your own home in some of the most innocent movies. We did not know except from a book which you were not allowed to read openly what the production of a child was all about. We could not and did not ask embarrassing questions because we were told that babies were found under the gooseberry bush. Modern children do not know what a gooseberry bush looks like but they do know where babies come from and more importantly how they got there. As queen Victoria said while in the throes of producing nine children that lived 'you just lie back and think of England.'

With all my purity of deed (not thought) I had at least three proposals of marriage during my stay at Radbrook. I knew I was going back to mother and Scotland eventually as I had no intention of becoming a wife or even residing in England. I was too young to contemplate marriage. Having just completed my lengthy impecunious studies my plan was to embark on the long journey of life in my chosen career and supply some money to the home front. The first part of my career was my appointment as head cook at Radbrook replacing Gill. It was quite strange as I had given in my notice to leave although I knew the promotion to Gill's post was available. My thought was that if they had wanted me to take over from Gill the Principal would have suggested that to me or even asked me.

After a few weeks the question was put to me as to why I had not applied for the now vacant post as head cook. I thought naively that if they had wanted me to be upped from assistant cook to head they would have asked me first instead of placing an advert in the catering magazine. The formula was patiently explained to me and the point was that all vacant posts in the education authority world had to be seen to be advertised fairly although an inside appointment was already on the mat for the post was mine for the asking. One did not do C.V.'s in these days at least I not only never had one but I was never asked to apply for one, never heard of such a thing but also never did one. I had the gumption to realise that if I accepted this promotion it would look good in my portfolio which would be enhanced by the fact that not only had I successfully completed my compulsory year out but also that I had stayed on for a second year underlining the fact that the powers that be had decided I was capable of and worthy of more responsibility in this promotion. Naturally the money was almost doubled. My vacant post as assistant cook was filled by Veronica (a Radbrook Junior student) who was not only a country and Salop lass born and bred but an instinctively wonderful baker and cook for whom her mother and her education at Radbrook College must swell with pride. Veronica and I became firm friends.

The marriage proposals were being carefully parried with my new found method of tactfully pretending not to understand, consequently my life was most enjoyable both at home in Denny and at work in Shrewsbury as I worked and rushed home for the college breaks at Christmas, New Year, Easter and the Summer Holidays.

. Perhaps I was beginning to think that this situation would always be with me as you do.!! Eventually in 1956 I proffered my notice again so that I could leave at the end of the college term. In the meantime Gill's brother, John, whom I had met at Gill's wedding in January that year, had become one of my friends. We had corresponded and met up a few times with Gill and Jack at dances etc. and at their farm and with others of their friends To all intents and purposes we were very much in love and it was a fantastic feeling. I remember yet the music at the end of the evening during the last waltz which I was dancing in John's arms. (Oh Johnnie! Oh Johnnie! How you can love!!)

By present day standards we would have homed to somewhere to be in bed together. But in 1956 nice girls did not succumb to these temptations no matter how strong the urge to risk the unthinkable; a pregnancy out of wedlock! The crescendo of this affair was mounting although I still had other casual boyfriends who took me out to country dance classes and cinema etcetera. John was in the Fleet Air Arm consequently he was absent quite a lot and he did not have a car (no one did) which meant we depended upon Gill and Jack for transport to meet during his leaves. John sent me nylons and other nice things which were not available in the U.K. Yes, although the rationing was over many things which you take for granted to-day had not reached our shores or shops.

Time passed most pleasantly and I could have stayed there for years but my Scottish blood was pulling me to mother and Scotland. I returned home in July 1956. There is no accounting for this home bond because the old homestead in Denny was a big bedroom divided in two plus a large sitting room cum eating room where my piano resided plus a scullery with my large gas cooker and the essential toilet and big 'wally' sink. That was it. That is for what I had left behind all these palatial large English residences and adoring fellows. A true proof of the eternal words 'be it ever so humble there's no place like home' I do not know to this day how you define 'home.' Some say home is where the heart is. Perhaps that is it; pity my heart had not been in England at that time. My brother and sister were both unmarried and mother was in Denny alone with us children! (If my father had lived everything would have been so different or would it? We would all have been farmer's wives or farmers). We all felt a certain need to stay with mother I think. As children are so selfish and self centred I am not sure if my reasoning is true. I dwell on this subject because of the harvest of marriage proposals I stacked into barns. I should have known the lean years would come.

Worse was to follow John sent me a beautiful, full china coffee set in the old colonial wooden tea chest (a something we never see nowadays although mother always had at least one or two of these as they were terrific for the packing of her glass and china for her ubiquitous flit tings) and he arrived on the doorstep of 6a East Borland Place, Denny not only to deliver it but to ask me to marry him. I was in a state of shock. I cannot remember what I said or how or why I refused. It must have been awful for him to have to make that long boring journey back to Shrewsbury/Ludlow with such a final rebuff and a broken heart to keep him company.

I do remember being anxious for John to leave in case mother found him there and came to some immoral conclusion. I thought I was quite a kind person. Maybe I was. We were reared so strictly and mother was such an unforgiving prude that I did not have the courage to arouse her disapproval apart from the standard I had set for myself. From the distance of fifty years on, and the knowledge of how the world and his wife have changed I can see it all through a glass darkly. I would have done it all so differently or would I? Life is full of cross roads as you will have found, I hope, and how to take the correct turning will always be a mystery. I may dwell on this later but suffice to mention that I met John in 2006, fifty years after that sad Denny episode, at his sister Gill's Golden Wedding. He looked terrific. He was still tall, dark and handsome, retired out of the police force which he had joined after the he left the fleet air arm when he got married in 1960 to his lovely wife who was with him that evening of course. My heart lurched and I felt like a teenager again. The entire past fifty years disappeared as in a dream. My world stopped there with John for a few moments while we spoke then, wham, 'take your seats for the dinner' and reality returned.

Boyd said he looked at me fleetingly and noticed that I had temporarily metamorphosed into a young girl in looks and demeanor as if by magic. For the next two months my life passed as if I was not in it. The parallel feeling can be seen through the eyes of Celia

Johnstone in the film 'Brief Encounter' where she sits and looks at her husband, her home life and all it entails as if she was an outsider looking at a stranger and in a strange land. Everything around me felt alien. I did not belong. I must have projected something of this to Boyd (Papa) because he decided quite soon after that that he would like to go back to Dunoon, actually in May 2006. Hence we put Sunart, our Isle of Skye house up for sale.

Back to Denny, the departure of John, the arrival of mother and the year still 1956. Mother seemed quite pleased with the coffee set so was I but I felt a heel for keeping it but would have felt a greater moron if I had thrown it back at him. I was taught to accept gracefully anything but blows whether I liked the article or not. Life at Denny soon evolved harmoniously with me working in the Prince's restaurant in Glasgow for Rio Stakis and the Stakis firm of restaurants. Only three at that time but Stakis grew to own a great part of Glasgow and eventually holdings in England as well as several other part of Scotland. He had the first Casino in Scotland located in Glasgow which was fantastic considering he had arrived in Scotland with a suitcase full of Cyprus lace from his mother just after the war.

Being a Greek Cypriot himself most of the Stakis staff was Cypriots and mixing of the races was strictly forbidden. This presented a small problem for me when the Cypriot boy Michael, in the dispense bar started to thrust his attentions on my good self. We all knew the house rules and I had no wish to be reprimanded or indeed dismissed by a Cypriot Boss for the unwanted, unsolicited amours of a Cypriot member of staff. I travelled by 'bus from Denny to Glasgow daily and at night I caught the last 'bus from Buchanan Street at approximately 11pm. The restaurant closed at 11pm at which time all the staff poured out on to the street and dear Michael offered to give me a lift home to Denny in his car. I guess he thought that the fact that he owned a car would impress me. Maybe it did but not enough.

I know that he followed the 'bus at least one night and was waiting for me when I alighted at Denny Cross to give me a lift down Broad Street. I accepted as gracefully as possible as I had no wish to be churlish and offend him. But I made it clear that it was a non starter in future.

My other faithful swain was the head chef George. He was Polish, married with children thus not of any interest to me. I was off in the afternoon from 3pm to 5pm. and as the journey from Denny to Glasgow took 1 hour in the bus I had to plan how I would or could pass these two hours as restfully as possible. Shopping was acceptable for one day per week but was an exhausting and expensive daily activity and as I was on my feet from 11am to 11pm in the restaurant I had to seek a more restful past time for these hours. I sometimes took in a movie at the plush cinemas and as there were several of these around the Prince's restaurant (like Odeon, Cosmo, Greens to mention but three). I could perhaps do two cinema afternoons per week without repeating shows. Both George and Michael found out where I went or followed me thus on one or two occasions I found George seated beside me in the dark in the cinema. I had to cut this intrusion in the bud as nicely as possible as they were my work mates and I wished to continue the friendship status without attachments and did so by going to the big stores like Coplands or Dalys or Hendersons. (They were sort of similar to Harrod's in London)

These salubrious Stores, similar to Mr Selfridges, had a mannequin parade or some similar entertainment in their restaurant on the top floor so now I would be found mixing with the ladies who did afternoon tea. This was quite an event and well patronised by ladies of leisure, the wealthy wives of business men from the suburbs meeting their friends after shopping for tea and chat also giving them the opportunity to view the next afternoon dress or evening dress for daughter or self from the comfort of the seat at the tea table. I had no intention of buying but I did enjoy the rest.

The tea was served by waitresses wearing black dresses and white frilly aprons and starched white caps trimmed with a velvet band. All the tables seated four but if one was alone like me I could join a table where two or three ladies were already seated or two or three ladies could join me if I was the only person at a table. This was acceptable by all the ladies and one was always made welcome and included in their conversation. If one wanted to be alone a book was quite useful to hide behind but I felt it to be too rude to use that prop. The tables were covered with crisp white linen damask tablecloths topped with a centre piece of the ubiquitous three tier silver cake stand. The bottom plate displayed the thinly sliced cucumber sandwiches, the middle plate held the scones and pancakes and of course the top plate was crowned with a selection of fairy cakes, French cakes, meringues and other succulent sweetmeats. We ladies were supplied by the waitress with a pot of tea, (in a silver teapot) a cup, saucer, teaspoon, a side plate with a side knife, cake fork and paper napkin. A paper napkin was a luxury and a bit ostentatious as we were just out of a war during which we were totally deprived of all paper articles except for limited news paper and hard crisp toilet paper in flat pack individually leafed for your economy and convenience.

At least in these surroundings I could escape the attentions of Michael and George but sometimes I pretended I was going into a store then shot out the back way and managed to reach a cinema undetected by my followers. This all added a spice to life which I thoroughly enjoyed as it was all quite harmless and I was not at any time rude to either of them so that both of them lived in hope of more than a friendship and continued a tenuous courtship by showering me with presents like boxes of chocolates and jewellery. (I still have a diamanté necklace, bracelet and brooch plus a marquisette bracelet and earrings that I know of maybe more in my jewel box to this day dating from the Prince's restaurant period 1956)

The chocolates I gave to David (my brother) as he was in Denny with me and as a student he was always hungry. (I tried to keep my slim figure.) David hoped that I would be able to hang on to these passions so that his supply of chocolates would continue and they did. Faithfully, every Friday, as George seemed to win at the races I benefited from his gains to the tune of a large box of chocolates or a larger box of chocolates. I guess he gave all his wages to his wife but he had other methods of making money apart from the gambling on horses. He could skin some money off the suppliers such as the butcher for example where a more inferior cut of beef can be supplied to the restaurant but the owner would be charged for the top cuts then the chef and supplier would pocket the difference between them with no harm done to the restaurant well not noticeably, also his wife would not be short changed financially through his amorous attentions and expenses incurred by his fruitless courting of myself.

At this time David and I used to host 'farewell' parties at 6a. To these we invited all our friends from Denny and Stirling and once we had included Dunoon in our home place we extended the boundaries to include Margaret Redman, Lennie Lochrie, and Boyd Dickson to mention just three. Unbeknown to me we had become the party place. To this day these friends remind me of the joy and happiness we generated in a period of suppressed night life and activities. Within ten years others were joining in on the party act but David and I remained the mould breakers according to the Denny and Dunoon public. The parties entailed the preparation of food. I made trifles, jellies, sausage rolls, sandwiches, vol-au-vents similar to the children's parties of today. Each person brought alcohol or soft drinks so the bar was set up with no great expense to the host and of course the essential record player for singing and dancing. That was it. No sex, no bed scenes, no stripping and of course no drugs. We all thoroughly enjoyed the good clean fun although we were perhaps a little tipsy by the end of the evening.

In May 1957 I left the Prince's Restaurant owned by Reo Stakis and went home to Dunoon. We still had the flat in Denny and sometimes journeyed back and forth from Denny to Dunoon. Now

I took an interim post as cook-caterer in the Wellington Hotel, Dunoon. My job was cooking for 25-50 resident and non residents guests for breakfast, lunch and dinner, doing weddings and other catering for that number all by myself including all the washing up. It was hard going but I was young well now 23 year old. As Dunoon was a popular holiday resort there were many activities and entertainments. Daisy had a dairy shop and mother had another dairy shop which they ran in tandem. The dairies were a seven day week and my job was a seven day week while David had a holiday, from University, job with one of the local fruiterers for whom he drove a van, helped in the shop and went to the fruit market in Glasgow at 5am most mornings. We were all exhausted when we reached home (Ardgour Dairy) for our break times which fortunately took place in a time stagger as there was only one couch (a moquette bed settee type) in the living room thus one of us was resting or asleep on this unfortunate piece of furniture throughout the day positioned with head down and feet up the back or wall.

At night we had a revival of energy and went out to Juno's Café (for the girls) or the Crown Hotel Bar (for the boys) and hence all on to the Pavilion Dancing until well after midnight. It was great. We met new people each Saturday night chose one with whom to forge a friendship for the week. As my hours were geared to afternoon off duties for three hours and off at night at 8pm roughly I was available to accompany one of these new boyfriends for afternoon bus tours, putting on the putting greens, tennis, swimming in the Lido. I met the local girls who were in the same game plan as me and we had some terrific evenings at Ardgour Dairy after the dances in a foursome or six some which included Margaret and Grace (both of whom I am in contact with to this day) plus the boys we met at the Saturday dance (mother and David slept in another house which we had in Cromwell Street so we were not disturbing anyone with our noise nor being disturbed by parental dictate.) When the week was over we went to the pier and waved a tearful farewell to our faithful swain of the past week while they were boarding the steamer to leave Dunoon while eyeing up the male talent which was disembarking from the steamer. At night we were off to the Pavilion again to repeat the strategy of the previous week. Sometimes we were heartbroken for an hour or two but mostly it was a great game and no one was hurt. The summer passed in this fashion.

I digress to mention that there were three tour bus firms all competing for the tourists who arrived by ferry all naturally without a car thus the buses were well patronised. Blue Line Buses, Silver Line Buses, Gold Line Buses. Roddy Campbell from the Isle of Lewis drove for Blue Line and that was how he met my sister Daisy whom she unfortunately married. Roddy,s sisters Effie and Peggy worked in the Esplanade Hotel as waitresses at this time too but they went to the teuchter dancing in the Masonic Hall as did Daisy and Roddy and a few of Daisy,s Gaelic choir friends plus all others mostly an older and highland clientèle. Even our Pavilion Dancing was frequented by married couples in their 30,s and 40,s who were keen on what we called modern dancing like quick-step, foxtrot, tango, Gay Gordon,s, pally glide, waltzes plus the now creeping infiltration of jive and rock and roll.

These tour buses took one for runs in the afternoon and in the evening. The evening runs usually ended at a village hall where a band would be playing for dancing. At these dances there was always tea and cakes not alcohol which makes it unbelievable to the youth of today that we could spend the whole night from 9pm to 1 or 2am with dancing, talking, drinking tea and having no alcohol or sex. There were also evening cruises on the steamers on the Clyde with again music and dancing. We had a wonderful time and I look back to these years with very very happy nostalgia.

By the October of 1957 I left the Wellington Hotel and took up the post as Restaurant Manageress in A.& F Reid fs, Gordon Street Restaurant opposite the Central Station in Glasgow. My boss was a Mr Durning but my immediate superior was Mrs Cassells who was lovely and we became great friends although I was there for only three months awaiting my posting to the Gas Board. I was in full charge of the catering side of the dining room at the opening of this new concept of continental catering. We did not serve fish and chips we were trying to educate the Glasgow public to eat healthily viz a viz open sandwiches or smorgasbord using greens, salads, nuts, pineapple, smoked salmon. Quite a culinary shock for the Glasgow eaters.

It was while there that I met Maverick who was a most stately, gentlemanly Dalmatian whose owner drove up to the restaurant door in a red open topped Jaguar sports car. Maverick reclined on the plush leather upholstery before and after his sojourn into the restaurant where he lay peacefully beneath the table.

When I left there to go to the Gas Board in George Square in Glasgow as a Home Service Adviser and Demonstrator in January 1958 I kept in touch with Mrs Cassells through thick and thin. She was such a super person and so good, kind and understanding in every way. We still use the alabaster lamp which she gave us as a wedding present forty three years previously. Much later in 1962 she gave me a highly pedigreed Dalmatian Puppy, son of Maverick which she had won in a competition. She lived in a council house in the Dalmarnock area of Glasgow and in these days council house tenants were not allowed to have a pet, added to that she was out all day so could not care for a dog properly. I loved him dearly and called him Bart because there was a t/v programme in which James Gardner played the part of twin gambling poker, playing brothers who were called Bart and Bret Maverick and as he was son of Maverick it seemed a natural title.

There were twelve of us taken on to be trained as Home Service Advisers for the Gas Board in January 1958. The training was quite strict not only from an ability to cook and sew, wash and iron to a high standard but also to have the ability to speak throughout all the processes to an audience of peers who knew as much if not more than

Will that ever be folk?

one did while presenting oneself to a high standard of grooming and smartness. While there I was in the Kelvin Hall in Glasgow picked for the team to demonstrate cookery and gas appliances be it gas cooker, gas fridge and even gas washing machine. During all this time I was homing to Denny but by May when we were all deemed capable enough we were sent out to a district of our own.

As convenience would have it I was given what I wanted that being a solo position in charge of all demonstrations and follow up calls for a Home Service Adviser with the Gas Board in Greenock. (Just across the water from Dunoon). Now I could travel home daily to Dunoon and to mother and as David was finished his University we were finished with the flat in Denny. The post in Greenock was great. I had my own little Austen A35 van allocated to me, the home service adviser, as my very own. I felt so proud and important. All the Gas Board technicians made great fun of me and my wee van. They thought I should upholster, carpet and curtain it as I kept it so pristine compared to the disastrous, smelly vehicles they had. I almost did. As I used it only for 4 hours daily they wanted to borrow it for part of the time. That was permissible as long as he did not leave her less that perfect.

It was there I met Pat Tosh and Pat Sweeney both of whom worked in the Greenock Gas Board office and are still special friends. Pat's husband Jim had a butcher's shop in Greenock and they lived in Port Glasgow. When I was doing a cookery demonstration at night I was unable to get home to Dunoon because the last ferry was at 6pm and even the wee private ferry called Ritchie's was at 9.30 but Pat kindly offered me a bed for the night with them. As Jim was surrounded by meats of all sorts every day I made sure that I had a succulent pudding or two of the sweet course variety to take home to him. I took my own linen and slept on a studio couch. (the like of that is never seen today) These studio couches were a very 60's style piece which could be a single bed, a double bed or a couch but in no way like a sofa bed or the old style bed settee. They were soft and comfortable.

My Dunoon life as reported earlier was back in full swing as I was in Dunoon each weekend from the beginning of 1958 and now in Dunoon every night where possible. We always frequented the Pavilion Dances and at one of these I met, Boyd Vernon Dickson (Papa to you).

I was progressing out of the dance hall on a Saturday night with Donnie McDonald as he had asked me to accompany him to a party at Lillian Day's who was running this said function for B.V.D's 24th birthday. I must presume B.V.D. was Lillian's current boyfriend. I was never one to split up any relationship no matter how serious or tenuous and I had not noticed him in the dance hall. I knew Donnie well from a boy/girl friendship angle, no more, no less, never was. I met up with Donnie outside the dance hall as arranged where the fellow beside him said in a general fashion or to Donnie in particular 'she's the one I wanted'. I naturally looked at the owner of this bold statement and saw that it was Lillian' boyfriend. He was emboldened by Johnnie Walker and stood there smiling broadly but Donnie and I rushed off before he could say any more.

I had to take Donnie home to Mother first to let her know what I was doing and where I was going as it was now Sunday. She was in Ardgour Dairy raking out the last dying embers of the fire in the black grate before retiring for the night to Cromwell Street. I asked permission to go to this party from midnight till the wee sma' hours and she agreed. Next morning she asked me 'where did you get that spotted faced youth'? Donnie was 18 and had the unfortunate teenage affliction of the eruptions of impurities on his face but apart from that he was quite handsome.

The party was great as expected and the company, dancing, music and drinking were up to the usual standard. Lillian was a party animal. I spent the night trying to keep sober (I was successful) because I was aware that B.V.D. was hell bent on trying to get

Will that ever be folk?

Donnie drunk so that he (b.v.d) would have to take me home instead of the boy I came with viz a viz Donnie. In the end I took Donnie home to his Aunt's house and put his key into the door, rang the bell and ran away fast before his Aunt would see me.

As was our custom we girls met up on a Sunday night at Margeret fs place or mine and repaired to Juno fs Café where we sat and drank iced drinks, knickerbockers glories or coffee, giving and getting an update of the previous evening while listening to the music on the juke box or casually sauntering over to put our own choice on the turntable while looking askance at the occupants of the other tables especially if a certain boy of interest was there. It was purely a boy meets girl situation or the hope of a boy meeting girl exercise and quite excitingly innocent. Then we went home and prepared ourselves for the weekly grind of making money.

Actually I think we all enjoyed our work. I know I did. By now I was travelling daily to Greenock to the Gas Board via the ferry from Dunoon to Gourock so I had to be up at 6.30am as the ferry was at 7.25 am. I had my dog to walk apart form get dressed. If I was up late then I used the ferry facilities for my hair and face embellishments and had tea and a roll in the tea room. At my office I collected my follow up calls from the gas fitters, planned my route, had tea with the other staff and set off in my little van with the gingham curtains to visit the people who had bought new Gas cookers, washing machines or fridges to check that they were satisfied and had no complaints. I asked them to sign a card and off I went happily to the next customer. If there was a complaint I tried to rectify it here and now. If it was too technical I reported it to the charge fitter. If it was an oven complaint I regulated the knobs then did a baking test, scones for top heating, pastry for bottom heating and Victoria sponge for correct all over heating. If my sample was successful then the customer was satisfied if not the fitter was called out or if required a new appliance was supplied. With my little van I could do 12 calls per morning and as the previous home service adviser did only 4 calls during the whole day I stopped at 10 or 12 so that the next girl would not have too many to aspire to thus my afternoons were spent trying out recipes to photograph for the gas board brochures or helping the girls in the showroom to sell appliances. I liked that as I could sharpen my sales skills.

I was my own boss and could have lazed around more but I loved to work and be busy. If I had a demonstration to do in the evening then I prepared all day for that and the next day I cleaned up my hamper, dishes, utensils and cooker. I was supposed to have a day off in lieu of each nightly demonstration but I always went to work just in case I was required but mostly because there was always something that needed to be done and I could help the girls like Pat Tosh and Pat Sweeney as I owed them so much by way of accommodation overnight and welcome hospitality in their homes whenever I was stranded on the Gourock side after the last ferry had gone.

My Dunoon evenings and weekends passed as eventfully as before and my travelling and working like wise but soon opportunity for a change loomed brightly in the form of a post as a teacher of Home Economics at Port Glasgow High School. My friendship with (papa to you) continued to flourish from the time I met him that fateful night at Lillian fs Party. We did have a casual date or two then he went off to sea. By some accident of fate his ship fs sailing was delayed for a few days so he rushed home from Liverpool to Glasgow and hence by ebus to Denny where he arrived at midnight only to find one of our parties in full swing. He dropped his seaman fs sailcloth sausage bag on the scullery floor and proceeded to wash himself at the kitchen sink just as if it was his home. I was mildly surprised but the jaws of the other guests did a quick drop and a double take. I tried my best to belittle the importance which was being given to the situation and handed him a towel with a Jane like master stroke then walked away. This surprise arrival of Papa and the fact that he seemed to be so at home with David and I created a rift between Willie Mackintosh and me. Willie and I were becoming quite cosy up to that point. In fact Willie was my invited partner although to make things look casual I had invited his brother Gow whom David and I knew well from the fact that they had been at Denny High School with David and now all were at Glasgow University plus the added meeting on the daily bus journeys from Denny to Glasgow which I explained previously. Willie was my boyfriend in Denny and as long as I could keep my Denny separate from my Dunoon all was well. Now the twain had met so Willie felt usurped and treated me with a certain chill from then on. I was not upset because even when Papa went back to sea I had other fish swimming around in the pools both in Denny and Dunoon.

I left the Gas Board in April 1960 and commenced my employment as a teacher on 18th April 1960. About that time all contact with the Denny flat terminated so mother must have sold it. David and I still kept in touch with our male and female friends in Denny, Dunipace and Stirling but from now on we had to meet in Glasgow or Dunoon. This was the beginning of a new chapter. Now I travelled daily between Dunoon and Gourock via the first ferry again but this time it was to go to Port Glasgow High School as a teacher of Home Economics. The ferry arrived in Gourock at 7.55am and I had a short 'bus run from there to the School which would have meant that I would have arrived by 8.15am. As I was not the head teacher I had minimal preparation to do before 9.am so my travelling companions Mat Carnegie and Jack Holmes who both worked for an American firm, I.B.M. (a few miles away from Gourock in Iverkip, the opposite direction from me) and the three of us repaired to a 'greasy spoon' type café near Gourock pier and beside my 'bus stop where we ate the most delicious freshly made bacon rolls and mugs of steaming hot tea.

At night in the summer the three of us plus Grace Paterson had a few highly competitive games of tennis. I also played tennis with Grace and another boy from the bank where she worked plus another casual boy friend Malcolm Mackay (an eighteen year old police cadet – I was by now 26 years old) I was writing to Papa all this time but life has to go on at home while the old salt is at sea. My social life was full of friends and acquaintances and dancing partners in Dunoon, in Denny, 'bus journey companions, Gas Board colleagues, ferry travelling companions plus my teaching colleagues at Port Glasgow High School (the Art Teacher Mrs Robb, Helen Fulton now Mrs Bernard Butcher in Derby as both she and her husband had become lecturers in Derby University as she had a 1st class Honors Degree in English and History, Ethel Reid, head teacher of Home Economics I was busy with my school work, night school work at the Greenock Women's Prison and at St Euphrasia's Convent near Bishopton where the Nuns looked after girls in need and care and attention. (The latter is now called the convent of the Good Shepherd from where 2 girls escaped in 2006 or 7 or 8 and jumped off the Erskine Bridge to their death.)

I taught these girls Cookery for 2 hours each Thursday night then stayed with Pat Tosh or someone like that. These girls worked for their food and accommodation by doing laundry, big time, all the bed linen, table linen and personal laundry for the passenger ships and liners which came up the river Clyde at that time apart from all the Convent laundry. The big ironing facilities they worked at were called calendars.

As for the Prison night school class I did in Greenock Women's Prison I was allowed to teach cookery to the first offenders only. Although they were not vicious some were really clever and full of guile like embezzlers. One had to be alert at all times. They were not allowed to have knives so most of the cooking was done by me in demonstration mode. I was locked in the room with the class but I had two burly, large lady wardens in with me guarding me and the door. I tried to make the lesson not only interesting but also good to eat so that my time with them brought not only a diversion from prison routine but also a treat of tasty food for the whole audience as I incorporated a few additional dishes that I had made earlier.(as in Blue Peter). Although I was well paid for these two night school classes I was not financially motivated. I loved doing them because the welcome was fantastic. The Convent girls always said 'God bless you miss' as I left and pressed an effigy of a saint into my hand. The prison women were allowed to help with the washing up and packing for me. It was actually wonderful and I felt quite privileged.

My social life was super too. I was still writing to Papa but sometimes he stopped writing to me and sometimes he came home from sea and went out with the lads or another girl like Anne MacArthur or Mairi Tinney without contacting me or making any arrangement to see me so there was no 'frat pin wearing' being done by me. I always had plan B and of course one or two other boyfriends like Kenneth MacArthur and Malcolm Mackay, both of whom were madly in love with me and proposed marriage several times. Malcolm was 9 years younger than me and I felt the gap would be too great. I thought also that his mother would think I was a baby snatcher. Both of them bought me a memento for my charm bracelet in the form of a policeman, an anchor and a ship's wheel instead of an engagement ring.

Kenneth was a year younger than me and he was at sea like Papa so it was easy to keep a friendship with both of the latter two going as long as they were not both at home on leave at the same time. Malcolm was the police cadet so he had to be kept at an arm's length, so to say, as he was there all the time and knew about the other two. Life was pretty hectic but great fun and at times I had to involve mother to get me out of a few sticky situations when two or more of my suitors were about to meet at my front door. One of the memorable occasions was when mother wanted to look at a house in Innellan and I said fine Kenneth with give you a lift when he arrives. It was a lovely sunny Saturday afternoon so she dressed in her culottes and sporty cavalry twill jacket. I rushed to answer the doorbell only to find it was not Kenneth but Papa standing there. I had a quick intake of breath, quickly gathered my composure and said we could speak more privately outside and ushered him towards the back garden where there was a couch on the grass awaiting the van to collect it for delivery somewhere. I left Papa sitting on the couch with his back to the door while I rushed to inform mother of the change of plan. Maybe now it will be Papa's car which will be the transport and as it was a two tone blue and grey Vauxhall Super Deluxe limousine mother decided to change her outfit to something like dress and coat. No sooner had she changed than Kenneth arrived so she re-donned the sporty wear. I managed to get Kenneth to take mother to Innellan but not before he had noticed the body sitting on the couch in the garden and made a point of telling me to chose there and then. I kept my cool and bent a few stories to suit the situation and get me off the hook of final decision time until mother had at least had her lift to Innellan.

Later that day was curtains for Kenneth. Well he made me decide. I had tried so hard to keep them both in the running and felt rather sad that this was now the end. I knew I would not ever marry Kenneth but he was a great friend, a useful partner, very kind and considerate, mother was most fond of him, I was by now a friend of his father, mother, and sister and he was well liked by my brother and sister in fact I had taken Kenneth to Lewis to stay with Daisy and Roddy and why not?

He was my friend and he was there at home at the time on leave so was free to take me wherever I wanted to go with the added quality of having a car. I was going to Stornoway anyway to see Daisy and he offered to take me there. Well I paid the fares but once on the island a car was a bonus and thus with Kenneth I had it all. I felt quite lost to have cut the chord and lost my friend. He just was not going to hang around any more. Papa was quite attentive but not overly so and he blew hot and cold constantly. I felt the draft as he was not as malleable as Kenneth but it was unfair of me to think that way. I cut and ran. At last Kenneth was free from me.

As long as one is not inflicted by dementia or Alzheimer's or Parkinson's we always have our memories.

Lightning Source UK Ltd.
Milton Keynes UK
UKHW010614090220
358415UK00001B/51